SEX
WITHOUT STRESS

A couple's guide to overcoming
disappointment, avoidance, and pressure

Jessa Zimmerman
MA, LMHC, CST

To all who know the pain
of this moment

May you know it no more

ADVANCE PRAISE FOR *SEX WITHOUT STRESS*

Whether being in a couple or working with couples, skill, perseverance and perspective are always important. Jessa Zimmerman, an expert in counseling couples, has written a much-needed book about couples. Her book is accessible and insightful. Her advice is never 'formulaic' but instead focuses on thoughtful and practical discussions about growing as a couple. I've wanted to refer to a book like this for a long time. So glad and not a moment too soon, Zimmerman has written it. I give it my highest recommendation!

—Sallie Foley, Director, University of Michigan Sexual Health
Certificate Program & Co-author, *Sex Matters for Women*

Jessa Zimmerman takes the reader through a straightforward and no-nonsense journey, highlighting the most common struggles that couples experience. This book identifies the top issues with which couples struggle: from defining what sex is or should be, desire discrepancies and differences in couples' sexual styles. She clearly maintains that it is essential for each partner to be accountable for themselves—and to each other— to follow the useful action steps she walks them through that are necessary to bypass avoidance, disappointment and pressure.

—Dr. Joe Kort, LMSW, Author & Speaker

A definitive resource that helps couples face and identify the pain of lost sexual intimacy. Jessa bridges the gap between sexual desire and sexual despair as she offers concrete methods to stop avoiding sex. Her techniques clearly outline ways to have "sex without stress" that are accessible to all couples, regardless of gender or sexual orientation. As a sex therapist, I highly recommend this book as it pursues reducing the pressure and finding the pleasure of sex.

—Edy Nathan MA, LCSWR, CST

Over the last 40 years, I have met many good couples struggling to become great, trying to recapture the passion they had when they first met. Sexual problems are common over a long-term relationship. Many couples avoid sharing their personal feelings about their sexuality, failing to address the personal barriers to recapturing that loving lust. Jessa Zimmerman's book addresses just that, helping couples who avoid sex to find transparency and willingness to share and explore oneself and each other's sexual map. *Sex Without Stress* can help your love life become great again.

—Dr. Kevin Seymour, Clinical Psychologist

ACKNOWLEDGMENTS

I am so grateful that I have so many people to thank for their contributions to this project.

Thanks to my partner, Kevin Makela, for his unending support. His continual votes of confidence, his unwavering belief in me, and his commitment to doing everything he could to help me get this done have been essential.

Thank you to my children. I love them more than anything, and they are the reason I do everything. A special thanks to Emma who provided the first (and very impactful) edit of this book.

Thank you to my coach, Jessica Butts. She promised me that if I wrote my book, I would get clear about my point of view and what I have to offer the world. I believe her now.

Thank you to Dr. Elizabeth Larson for introducing me to the concept of the Giver/Receiver exercise.

Thank you to my editor, Joshua Moro. He has done an amazing job of making the book so much better without diluting my voice or my message at all. In fact, by some sort of magic, his work has made them somehow even more mine.

Thank you to all the clients who have shared their stories, their pain, and their journey with me. They have inspired me in my work. This book is for them and for all the others that have known heartbreak in their sex lives.

CONTENTS

CHAPTER 1

___

Help Is Here: An Introduction

The most effective and powerful way to develop as a person and to change your relationship is to make the changes required to transform your sex life. That is why, from the beginning, I focused my therapy practice almost exclusively on working with couples and their sexual issues. Subsequently, I've assisted hundreds of couples in their work to reconnect intimately, emotionally, and sexually. I have been granted access to the inner workings of relationships and sex in a way few people ever experience. Over years of dedication to this field, I have developed ways to think about sex (and what's important about it) that create permission, freedom, and lightness in a relationship instead of heaviness and pressure. My practical exercises help people learn how to bring these ideas to fruition and apply them in their sexual lives. This is what I will share with you here.

Are you avoiding your sex life? I want to help.

If you've picked up this book, I imagine that you are unhappy about the state of your sex life. Perhaps in your relationship, sex is not working well. You love your partner, and you know sex matters, but sex has become a source of hurt, doubt, and confusion.

I also imagine you're anxious about confronting the topic of sex with your partner. You have no idea what you'll find or where the conversation will go. It's scary when you feel like sex isn't working. It often causes you to doubt yourself, your partner, and your relationship. Frequently, it's the thing keeping you awake with worry at 4 a.m. The human tendency is to avoid whatever scares us, so I imagine you and/or your partner are avoiding sex at this point. You're not happy, your partner's not happy, you can't talk about it productively, and the problems are palpable between you. This is the proverbial elephant in the room, and it is crowding out the positive parts of your relationship.

There is a way forward: you and your partner can get to a place where you'll enjoy your sex life. If you both want an intimate connection, then you can absolutely create it. That's probably another reason you've picked up this book. You know you want to be more than just roommates. You no longer want to feel lonely in bed with your partner, with that invisible, impenetrable wall between you. You don't want to repeat the awkward dance around having sex (or not having sex). You don't want to keep putting on the charade and continue living in a world where you don't enjoy your sex life. You don't know how to make it better, but you do know something needs to change. You still have at least a slight sliver of hope that there is something you can do that will make a difference. So you find yourself here, with this book. I want to help you do exactly that—get on a path where you and your partner can feel good about the state of your sex life, instead of feeling sadness, shame, frustration, confusion, doubt, and dread.

Since you are reading this, you have already shown you are willing to do something with that sliver of hope. You have hope in the possibility that things can improve. Embrace that hope. Believe that things can be good. Know that by adjusting your expectations, you will feel lighter. Sex can feel easy—and even playful. From where you are now—and this is vital to success—you must be willing to have the type of honest and open conversations that are the hardest part of this process. These conversations with your partner (and conversations with yourself) are a soul-searching reckoning about what's happening between you and your role in the dilemma. Can you commit to that? You've got to go on faith, at least in the beginning, by not knowing if your relationship can bear the weight of the process. But, I promise you, things won't get better on their own. What do you have to lose?

Who is this for?

I have written this book to help great couples—couples just like you—who wish their sex lives were great, too. What makes you a great couple? When at least some of these apply:

- You are still friends, even best friends.
- You manage something well together: you co-parent successfully, you manage your money, or you are cooperative partners in the home.
- You can still have fun together.
- You have a great relationship, separate from sex.
- You can talk about most things.
- You share a basic kindness and decency with each other.

This is not to say the two of you never quarrel, or that there aren't some problems in your relationship. But to get the most out of this book, you will need to have a solid foundation. If you have goodwill, love, and respect but don't know what to do to address your sex life, this book can help.

If this doesn't sound like your relationship, though, it may not be time to use this book. John Gottman, a famous researcher of marital stability, writes about what he calls the four horsemen of the apocalypse: defensiveness, stonewalling, contempt, and criticism. These behaviors are good indications of bigger issues in your relationship that will need to be addressed before you can work as a team to tackle your sexual issues. Find a good therapist and get some help, so you can be honest about your issues and learn how to interact as allies. If you do not feel good about the person you are or the person you're with, it's going to be difficult to change your situation—because to transform your sex life, it is more effective if you work together.

What do I know?

My journey to become a sex therapist grew out of my own struggles in a marriage that went terribly wrong. Things were great at first, as they are for a lot of people. Sex was easy and important to both of us. We shared interests, we had plenty of time together, and we really didn't have any stressors in our early life together to create emotional challenges. It was, of course, the honeymoon period, when everything seems simple. I'm sure neither of us imagined it would all come crashing down in the future. Who gets married, at least the first time, with any sense of how hard it is?

Once we had kids, there was stress on the relationship. That's when our differences, our inability to work together, and our struggle to collaborate were revealed. Those qualities had never really been tested before, and our relationship didn't do so well on that test when our children arrived. This, combined with a persistent pain I experienced during sex for months after the birth of our daughter, was a perfect storm. Since neither of us knew how to talk about what was happening, it went downhill from there.

In general, I tried to pretend everything was okay. But I couldn't stop the thoughts from flooding my mind in the early morning hours. I continued to experience a terrible dread that my relationship was in a bad place and might not be savable.

I felt embarrassed to be failing so badly. I grew up in a sex-positive household. My family was open about the topic of sex, and sex was discussed as something normal, positive, and healthy. It was clear my parents shared a happy, intimate life. They were happily married for 52 years, until my mother died. Yet even with knowledge about sex and the model of my parents' strong, lifelong, intimate relationship, I was completely ill-equipped to manage sex, intimacy, and cooperation with my husband.

With each passing year and with the addition of two more children into our lives, the tension in our relationship grew to the point where it was palpable. Sometimes we'd explode in a fight, but neither of us handled that well, either. I would pretend to be asleep when he came to bed. I was exhausted, anxious, and unable to handle what was happening. I didn't understand exactly why I didn't want sex, and I was overwhelmed by the complexity of our relationship problems. I knew he was hurting in our relationship, too, and I felt guilty. Yet, I did nothing. I was afraid we couldn't fix it. I was ashamed, I felt like I was failing, and I didn't know where to start. The marriage that had seemed so easy and joyous at the beginning, with the man I had chosen to have and to hold and raise children with, ended because we didn't confront our problems and didn't get therapy until it was too late to prevent our divorce.

The end of my marriage brought the necessity and opportunity to forge a new career. Although it seemed daunting to undertake graduate school, build a private therapy practice, and transition to life as a single mom of three, I knew enough to follow my heart. I was always the person that other people found "safe" to talk to, and I was passionate about helping people.

Deciding to become a therapist, I knew from the beginning that I wanted to focus on working with couples. I wanted to understand what makes relationships work and keep others from enduring the same fate of my marriage. I wanted to unlock the secrets of successful marriage that I couldn't learn just from watching my own parents. My master's program was incredible because it focused on personal growth and interpersonal experiences with the other members of my cohort. It was designed to challenge us as people and to create opportunities to change how we interacted with others to have more open and honest relationships. It showed me my challenges with intimacy and taught me how to achieve success in relationships, both intimate and otherwise. I met my current partner during that time, and we applied what I was being taught about openness, honesty, confrontation, and boundaries. I was able to take the concepts I was learning about healthy relationships and put them into practice. My partner and I have built our relationship strong from the beginning.

While I still have my own "messes," I do know a lot about how to keep the relationship healthy. I no longer avoid issues; I speak up when something needs to be addressed. I hold myself accountable, and I also challenge my partner to do the same. I work to be honest about my thoughts and feelings, even when it isn't to my advantage. I advocate for my needs, yet I strive to remain flexible and giving to ensure that I can meet my partner's needs. I'm willing to stretch beyond my comfort zone. I care for my emotional state and my reactivity when things are difficult so that I can stay grounded and respond honestly and constructively. I don't say these things to brag; I share this to illustrate the kinds of changes you can make. These are the kinds of skills I want to help you develop through the process described in this book. These also happen to be the skills that allow you to transform your sex life.

Early in my training, an instructor gave a seminar about her work as a sex therapist. She described how most of her cases involved grief and loss work. This notion of grief and loss entangled with a problematic sex life hit me square in the gut. Instantly I could relate to how people suffer when they struggle with sex. I know how vital our intimate connections are; it is a loss when they aren't working. We grieve. It feels extraordinarily painful. We feel hopeless and alone. I knew in that moment, sitting in the seminar: I was going to be a sex therapist. I decided soon after to undertake the extensive training to become nationally certified through the American Association of Sexuality Educators, Counselors and Therapists

What will you learn?

You are going to learn about how people get stuck exactly where you are and why it's such a common problem. You're going to learn how to think about sex and what kinds of expectations set you up for success. You will begin to understand what kind of baggage you bring to your relationship and its impact on your sex life. You will also see what your role is in the problems and what you need to do to change your part. You're going to learn to transform your sex life. In fact, working on the sex problem is going to positively affect the rest of your relationship. When you master what it takes to improve your sex life, you're set up for success in the other areas of your partnership as well.

This book follows the same structure and path that I take with my therapy clients:

Create understanding

- Understand how disappointment, avoidance, and pressure become a cycle
- Uncover and adjust your unrealistic expectations
- Change your beliefs about how sex and relationships work

Figure out what's going on and what's your part

- Learn to talk with your partner about your issues
- Unpack your baggage
- Discover what kinds of issues are complicating your sex life
- Deconstruct your unique dynamic around having (and not having) sex
- Create your individual action plan about what you need to change

Take action to change your sex life

- Learn the exercise that you'll use to create change
- Put insight into action with my 9-phase plan
- Resources, now and in the future

At the moment, you are stuck in a negative cycle, feeling things like disappointment, sadness, fear, frustration, and loneliness. But there truly is a way to escape that cycle to create a sex life that feels easy, joyful, pleasurable, and even playful. It's probably hard to imagine sex being anything but serious and stressful (if you can imagine having sex at all), but you can work with your partner to completely transform how you interact in and around sex. No matter how stuck you feel, there is a way to move forward. I want this book to help you change your sex life, connect with your partner, and look forward to intimacy rather than avoid or dread it. The first step in the process is to sort through this mess you are in now: understanding the Avoidance Cycle and how it works.

A few disclaimers

I have created several example couples, based on the stories and experiences from clients over the years. These couples are composites of the situations, details, and feelings that are common when people are dealing with sexual issues. You may feel like I am describing you specifically, but that's because I've found that the issues, themes, and even statements people make are common among couples struggling with sex. You will get to follow their journey throughout the book as they go from feeling stuck and hopeless to finding joy and ease in their sex lives.

I make every effort to use inclusive language throughout this book. I affirm every sexual orientation, gender identity, relationship structure and consensual sexual behavior, and I hope that is clear in my writing. This book is for couples. All couples. And it is meant to address sexual avoidance between any two people. I do not assume you are monogamous, straight, able-bodied, identified with your assigned gender—or any other particular trait. If you find any instance of less inclusive language or assumption, it is unintentional, and I apologize. My intent is to include everyone.

SECTION 1:

SET THE STAGE FOR SUCCESS

CHAPTER 2

The Sexual Avoidance Cycle

Despite the common belief that "sex is supposed to be fun, easy, and natural," a surprising number of people struggle with it. If you are having problems in your sex life, you are not alone. In my practice, I have seen young couples who haven't consummated their marriage, who struggle with sexual pain, or who argue about their different levels of sexual interest. I've seen middle-aged people who are dealing with stress and responsibilities overtaking their relationship, who have lost interest in sex, or who have gotten complacent and bored in their sex life. There are older couples who struggle with sexual dysfunction, are feeling the effects of disease and its treatment, or are just now beginning to talk about what they want out of their sex life. This isn't a complete list, of course. This is just a sample of the kinds of sexual concerns experienced by so many people. People like you. People like me. And people who don't realize that problems with sex are commonplace.

Struggles in your sex life can make you sad and anxious—especially if they happen often. If you aren't having sex, or at least not as much as you want, you may feel inadequate, as well as disappointed. If sex doesn't seem to go well when you do have it, the result leads to feelings of disappointment, or worse, failure.

And because it is human nature to avoid difficult and anxiety-provoking feelings, you may find yourself avoiding sex altogether:

having it, talking about it, and doing anything to change it.

In general, once you start to avoid something, your anxiety about it gets worse. It becomes harder and harder to approach whatever it is that you're avoiding. You start to feel pressure building up and bearing down on you. This compounding pressure only adds to the anxiety, creating a downward spiral of deeper and more ingrained sexual issues. Feelings of disappointment, failure, and inadequacy lead to avoidance. Avoidance creates increased anxiety and pressure. Heightened pressure just makes it harder to have a fulfilling sexual encounter, creating more feelings of disappointment, failure, and inadequacy.

Disappointment. Avoidance. Pressure. This is the Avoidance Cycle, and it is a vicious one, so it's important to discuss each of these experiences separately.

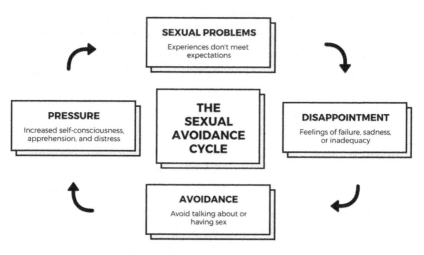

Sex feels disappointing.

Feelings of disappointment are the most common cause of the Avoidance Cycle; they kick off the whole process. Different couples will tolerate sexual struggles to different degrees, but it's common to start avoiding sex when bad feelings about it occur more frequently.

Sex can feel disappointing for many different reasons. You may have unrealistic expectations (although you may not realize they're unrealistic), leaving you sad and afraid when reality isn't living up to your ideal. You may have the unfounded idea that sex should be spontaneous, that men should last a long time, that women should orgasm through penetrative sex, or that penetration is the only sex that counts. These are a few common errant expectations, and there are many more. Every time you have sex that falls short of your expectations, it can feel like a failure, diminishing your confidence for the next time. Sex can feel disappointing because of what *is* happening instead of what *isn't*. You may see things about yourself or your partner that dishearten you. No matter where the disappointment originates, it leads you to feel more sad and anxious. It reaches the point where every sexual encounter holds the weight of the world, because each time is a test you expect to fail. Eventually, the survival of your relationship seems to hang in the balance. It feels like you are risking everything each time you have sex, depending on what happens during and afterward.

If sex isn't easy or natural, you may assume there is something wrong with you, your partner, or your relationship. You may worry that you're with the wrong person or that you are broken. Worries consume your thoughts, and you begin to question everything. The worries don't go away during sex. In fact, the worries tend to be magnified during sex, leaving you unable to be present with your partner. Inevitably, you wonder if your relationship is doomed.

When you're having sexual problems, it is common to worry about how your partner is feeling, both while having sex and in general. You may feel guilty about your sexual struggles because you want your partner to be happy. During sex, you spend time on your partner's "side of the court," trying to read whether they are pleased and what they want. For the most part, you are not allowing yourself to think about or pursue what *you* want because sex feels fragile and fraught with tension. You are vigilant during sex instead of getting to enjoy it. "Is this one of the times that will go pretty well, and I get to feel relief?" "Can the two of us 'check off the box' and feel like we're off the hook for a while before the pressure mounts again?"

The walls seem to close in. The space around sex gets smaller and tighter, constricting until it feels like there is no room to move or change.

You begin avoiding sex.

When sex seems to fail, when you feel disappointed afterward, when it ends in tears, sex begins to feel risky and negative. Sex is not the positive, enjoyable experience you hoped for, or that you may have shared with your partner in the past. Before you have any sexual problems, it's hard to imagine that having sex will ever seem negative or difficult. But now sex has become an increasingly negative experience: the more disappointing sex is, the more you end up avoiding it.

One of you is probably adept at missing the opportunities to have, or even to talk about, sex. It's common to make yourself busy in the evening or to fall asleep earlier than your partner. Perhaps you say, "I'm exhausted" at bedtime almost every night to signal that sex is off the table.

One or both of you may deflect any comments about sex or any bid to have sex. You may act like you're oblivious to the comments or actions—going on as if they never happened or that they mean something else. Or you use humor to respond to a genuine attempt to deal with the subject, effectively telling your partner that you're not going to take it seriously.

Perhaps you or your partner take those attempts to address sex and steer towards a fight, instead. You put the focus on your partner's level of sexual desire, high or low, or how sex is initiated, instead of addressing the fact that you're not having it. Or maybe you maneuver any mention of your sex life into a fight about a completely different topic, driving the conversation even further away from the subject of sex.

These techniques enable you to avoid addressing what's happening (or not happening) in your sex life. Indeed, there may be real issues to "fight" about—concerns about your relationship that need to be dealt with—before you're going to want to have sex with your partner. Those topics will need to be addressed. However, if you stage these fights instead of having a conversation about sex, you are creating even more problems. These are diversion tactics, a way to avoid saying, "I know we're not having sex, and I have some good reasons that have to be addressed so that we can make progress on our sex life."

The pressure mounts.

Avoiding your sexual problems doesn't make them go away. You might experience a brief respite once the subject of sex seems to be off the table. But unless you and your partner are both content in a sexless, sex-limited, or sexually problematic relationship, you can't escape the knowledge that at least one of you is unhappy. Even if you manage to put it out of your mind for a while because your partner isn't bringing it up, sex is right back at center stage as soon as you have your next heart-to-heart (or fight) about it. Even if there are no outward signs that either of you is thinking about sex, you think about it. A lot. More and more as time goes by. The thoughts start to monopolize your mental energy.

Avoidance creates pressure. Pressure comes from the belief that you should be having sex more often than you do. It comes from one person wanting sex while the other doesn't. It comes from the energy it takes to avoid the subject. Additionally, once your frequency of sex decreases due to avoidance, there is more and more pressure that the encounters you *do* have should go well. And when sex doesn't go well again (and again), the whole cycle amplifies. This is when you wonder if things will ever get better.

The pressure is becoming an ever-increasing presence in your relationship. You end up with that elephant in the room—suffocating any chance you have to enjoy sex together, to ever feel like it's successful. You are stuck in your head the whole time. You're certainly not connecting with your partner. This pressure can also manifest itself in other ways, like sexual dysfunction. It's not surprising that it's difficult to get aroused in such a state, much less reach an orgasm. Things are getting worse and you are getting...desperate? Resigned? Devastated?

So this is where you are. Your expectations aren't met. You feel disappointed. You start to avoid sex. Your sense of pressure increases. You have a harder time enjoying sex. And round and round you go. Once you're trapped in this cycle, it's hard to see any way out.

Fear can keep you from moving forward. Anxiety and avoidance rob you of the chance to improve your partnership and your sex life. Don't let the cycle consume you any longer. Your paralysis in the face of fear is what feeds the cycle. You're caught in the vortex of swirling feelings of inadequacy, disappointment, failure, hopelessness, pressure, and anxiety. As long as you stand still in the middle of all that, you can't escape to the other side, where it's light, playful, relaxing, and free. Instead of avoiding the things that scare you, you need to confront these issues, so you can move past them.

There are ways to heal, transform, and adapt to the complexities of your sexual situation. This book is about giving you the framework and the tools to make your sex life better. Before I talk about how you're going to change your sex life, I need to take a teaching moment and give you some basic information that will set you up for success. The first thing I want you to understand is that your expectations are the root of the problem.

———

Before you proceed, I want you to meet some people that illustrate some of the many ways couples get caught in the Avoidance Cycle. These are the couples that serve as examples throughout the book. You're going to check in with them as they move through the process I've designed to help you escape the Avoidance Cycle and recreate your sex life. They are varied in age, gender, and sexual orientation. Their family and sexual histories are different. Some of the people have sexual dysfunction; others don't. The types of issues and influences that affect their sex lives are all over the map. But they all struggle in the cycle of disappointment, avoidance, and pressure. Each couple feels completely stuck. None of them can imagine a time when sex might be easy or consistently enjoyable. But you will see as you read further in the book, each couple comes to understand exactly what's playing out between them and what they need to change to improve their relationship and sex life. Each couple completely transforms how they think about sex, what happens during sex, and how they feel about it. They move past being stuck and on to a place where they are happy and fulfilled.

Carol and Todd

Carol and Todd are a couple in their early 60s, empty nesters who have been married for more than 35 years. They're in pretty good shape, active for their ages. As they near retirement and begin thinking about how they'll spend their "golden years," they realize they want to address their sex life even though they haven't been talking openly about the problems they're having.

Todd struggles with erectile dysfunction. They have spent a long marriage together equating sex with penetration, so now that intercourse has become difficult, they don't know what to do. He visited the doctor and has a prescription for Viagra; it works some of the time. When Todd started to need actual physical stimulation to get erect about a decade ago, Carol saw that as a lack of interest in her. When younger, he would just be hard and ready to go. She had taken that as proof that she was attractive and that he wanted her. It wasn't until he naturally started needing more stimulation that it became apparent she'd made this association. So, as he needs more time and touch to get going, she sees this as a sign he is losing interest in her. This reveals her basic insecurity that she isn't attractive anymore.

It doesn't help that she has other factors complicating her ability to feel desirable and attractive. Carol is a breast cancer survivor and underwent a double mastectomy, chemotherapy, and radiation treatment a few years ago. Not only were her breasts removed, but she is also dealing with the ongoing effects of menopause. These changes to her body (and the impact of these changes on her sense of her feminine sexuality) have left her reeling. She is self-conscious about her scars, and she worries that her chest is a put-off for Todd. She isn't lubricating like she used to, partly due to hormonal changes and partly due to everything going through her mind. Todd is tentative about exploring her changed body, not knowing how she feels about it. Neither of them knows what to do now when it comes to sex. They both miss the way it used to be before cancer and the ED. Back in the day, they had a straightforward sex life that didn't take much work. They are facing losses (of sexual functioning and unmet expectations) every time they have sex. Every sexual encounter feels terrible to both.

Beth and Yara

Beth and Yara are a married couple in their 40s who have been together for almost 10 years. Sex has been a little challenging from the beginning and has gotten much more so in the last 4 or 5 years. They rarely talk about the problem, and when it comes up, they both end up feeling hurt and defensive.

As a result, they mostly avoid talking about sex and fight about other things instead. They always seem to have something that needs be talked about and worked out before they can even begin to address their sex life. They have issues about jealousy (how time is being spent and with whom). There are issues around job stress and who brings how much of that stress home. There are issues about pot and alcohol use and who is using how much and how the other feels about it. They go around in circles on all these various topics. But they never get around to talking about how rarely they have sex, how poorly sex seems to go, and how bad they feel about it.

Because sex has become a loaded topic, Beth avoids sex by keeping busy in the evening, stretching out her tasks to fill up the space before bedtime. Because she makes it take so long to get her stuff done, she doesn't sit down to "unwind a little" until Yara is ready for bed. She can then appear completely reasonable in wanting a bit of time to watch TV, effectively eliminating the chance for sex at bedtime. They are getting more and more distant as time goes on. They live separate lives, each busy with their own activities and commitments. The evenings are spent in front of the TV, but they don't even do that together most of the time. They are both unhappy but have largely resigned themselves to this existence.

Beth is struggling with feeling no desire for sex. She is entering perimenopause, and her body is not responding to sexual touch the way it used to. It seems to take forever to get aroused, if she even can, and she feels bad about that. She feels broken, like she doesn't work anymore. And that sense of brokenness (like something is fundamentally wrong with her) kills any desire she might have had for sex. She also has a hard time quieting her mind and letting go of distractions during sex. This makes their encounters even more difficult.

Yara is still interested in sex. In fact, she is coming alive to sex in a new way. She has had sexual interest in men throughout her life, as well as sexual experiences with men when she was young. She doesn't label herself as bisexual, since she is only interested in acting on her sexual interest with women at this point. She was confused about her sexual orientation and how she would identify when she was younger. Now, she is feeling more comfortable flirting and engaging her sexual energy with both men and women. This upsets Beth.

They struggle a lot with their desire discrepancy (in-depth details on desire discrepancy in Chapter 7). Beth will try to avoid sexual situations, and Yara doesn't want to put Beth on the spot. When they do become sexual at all, Beth will often criticize Yara for being sexual or assertive, trying to back her off so Beth won't feel exposed in her own sense of inadequacy. She will often deliver a subtle but cutting comment that will crush Yara, and their encounter will fizzle. Given how bad it feels to both, they largely avoid the topic and will go months without even trying to be sexual.

Jenny and Rich

Jenny and Rich are a couple in their 30s who have been married for 8 years and enjoy a good relationship in many ways. They are both kind and thoughtful people, and they have two young kids, keeping them busy. Jenny and Rich co-parent well and tend to be on the same page about most of the parenting decisions. That is less true about other areas of their life.

The two have lingering resentment over household chores and duties. Jenny feels like she's got the mental load of managing the household and the kids, and she hates having to ask repeatedly for Rich to step up and take the lead on some of it. Rich feels unappreciated for the extra hours he puts in at work to maintain their lifestyle, and he doesn't understand why Jenny seems so stressed out all the time. They each struggle to deal with conflict, so they largely avoid it until Rich explodes in frustration. Their mutual resentment and their lack of skills in addressing hard topics mean they struggle to work as a team. They also fight about sex. They have the same fight about twice a year, where Rich expresses frustration with their sex life, and Jenny gets defensive.

In between these biannual arguments, they don't address their sexual issues directly. Instead, they argue about sexual initiation. Jenny has said in the past that she doesn't like him just asking for sex and only touching her when he wants sex, so Rich tries to touch her and have some intimacy outside of the bedroom to set the stage for later. For example, he will try to initiate some physical intimacy by touching or kissing Jenny while she is in the kitchen. But then Jenny gets mad at him for interrupting her or not seeing that she is busy loading the dishwasher. She keeps the conversation focused on his initiation tactic, effectively boxing him into a corner where there is no way to do it right. This kind of conflict helps them avoid talking about how bad their sex life has become.

Rich wants more sex than Jenny. In fact, at this point, she doesn't want any at all. She has been the person less interested in sex all along, and she has spent quite a long time having sex because she thinks she should. At first, this worked okay. But she's gotten more frustrated because he seems content to have sex that is more focused on him. She is out of touch with what she wants in sex, and it doesn't seem to matter to him. He'll ask about what he can do for her, but he'll quickly move on when she doesn't have an answer. As she gets less and less into it, he gets upset.

Jenny hasn't felt desire in years, but she's been having sex out of a sense of obligation for a long time. She has finally hit a wall and is unable to keep doing that without feeling like she is giving herself away or compromising her integrity. They have hit a stalemate since they have not dealt with her lack of sexual desire to begin with. Her libido is affected by the anti-depressants she is on, but it is also affected by her long history of not thinking about what she wants and constantly trying to keep everyone else happy.

As Jenny has stopped just going along with sex, Rich feels rejected. He's resented being the sole initiator for sex for quite a while. Now, his confidence, his feeling of being desirable, and his sense of connection with her have plummeted. As they go longer periods of time without having sex, he is feeling hopeless and lost. He is also confused and hurt to realize she hasn't wanted to have sex. He could tell that sometimes she was more into it than other times, but he hadn't realized the degree to which she'd been faking an interest. Now that it has all come out, he has stopped initiating sex, and she largely avoids the subject because she doesn't see how it can improve.

Tom and Grant

Tom and Grant are in their 30s and in a young, two-year relationship. They are considering getting married but have concerns about their sex life. Sex quickly became problematic in their relationship, partly because neither of them know how to talk about it. Grant is questioning whether they are compatible because of their struggles. Each time they try to have sex, he is on high alert for signs of whether it's working or not. Tom is aware of Grant's vigilance, of course, so sex just feels stressful to him. At this point, when Grant brings up sex, he sees fear in Tom's eyes instead of desire.

Tom and Grant both tend toward being passive in the relationship, each wants the other to be assertive and take control. Neither has had much experience with penetrative sex. Tom has had some, but it's only happened with partners who were experienced and knew what they were doing. Grant hasn't had any. They both believe that penetrative sex is the "right" kind, so they both feel bad about their sex life since they aren't sharing that (though they both enjoy oral and manual stimulation and don't struggle with those activities). They are both interested in exploring penetration, but each thinks it should come naturally and that their partner should be the one to both know what they are doing and to make it happen.

Tom knows Grant is constantly evaluating the state of their sex life. Tom has developed erectile dysfunction due to the sense of pressure he has around each sexual encounter. Every time Tom struggles to get an erection, Grant takes it as a sign that their sex life is doomed and gets emotional and upset. Their sexual encounter comes to a dramatic halt, putting more pressure on the next time. Every time it goes that way, they end up distant and wrapped up in their own emotional wounds instead of connecting with each other.

At this point, they have fallen into a pattern of only joking about sex. Grant suggests sex but uses a silly, joking way of bringing it up that makes it easy to ignore. First, this type of silliness isn't sexy to Tom. Second, silliness about sex also signals that Tom can just joke back. Neither of them is forced to address the lack of sex in their relationship in a serious way. Grant protects himself by joking. If he doesn't make a serious request, Tom's lack of interest doesn't feel as much like rejection. Tom feels better because jokes keep the topic of sex lighter and less serious. Both know they aren't having sex and that they joke about it to avoid talking about the problems.

CHAPTER 3

Your Expectations Are the Problem

Remember how I said the Avoidance Cycle starts with disappointment? Disappointment is all about your expectations. It is the literal definition of disappointment: the feeling of sadness or displeasure caused by the non-fulfillment of one's hopes or expectations. Your expectations are the problem. Your expectations of yourself, your partner, and what sex is supposed to be and look like. The ideas in your head often overshadow your experience. They become the measure of your sexual success or failure.

Every time you feel like a failure, like something is wrong, or like you are inadequate, you will be less inclined to approach sex again. Holding yourself to an arbitrary standard, no matter where it comes from, is a buzz kill. Holding yourself to a standard that is grounded in your integrity and core beliefs is important, but you may withdraw if you aren't living up to what you expect of yourself. As soon as you feel like you need to perform, to be a certain way, or for certain things to happen, you leave the present moment and sit in judgment of yourself, your partner, and your sexual interaction. If you are meeting your expectations, sex is probably working—for now. But since so many expectations are arbitrary and unrealistic, you set yourself up for feelings of failure at some point in the future.

Expectations are informed by your history and culture.

You may or may not know where you developed a lot of your expectations. Over time, you have developed ideas about how sex is "supposed" to work. You have ideas about what to expect from your partner and ideas about how conflict should be dealt with or avoided. Your family and your past relationships have taught you a lot about these things, and most of it goes unquestioned until you take the time to examine it. You will get the chance to do that in the next section of the book.

Your expectations are also framed by culture. Think about how sex has been portrayed around you: in the media, school, sex education classes, and peer groups. You receive a lot of information from all these places, and you weave it together to create a picture of sex and sexuality. Sometimes these messages have been loud and explicit. Sometimes sex has seemed almost invisible, and no one was talking about it. Either way, your brain puts together a picture of how sex works, what it means, and how you are supposed to feel about it. You build an image of what to expect. By the time you started to be aware of sex and were becoming a sexual being, what were you expecting? What specific ideas did you form about what sex should be?

Pornography shapes your expectations.

I can't talk about sexual expectations without talking about pornography. Like other movies that feed us an image of what sex can or should look like, pornography can have a big impact on how we picture sex. Pornography has changed forms over the years, and it's much more pervasive than ever. Decades ago, you might have found someone's stash of magazines somewhere and gotten a view of people's bodies, sexual arousal, and sex itself. Other, racier magazines and video tapes showed you stories about how sex went in the imagination of their creators. Now you can be exposed to a huge variety of video material at your fingertips. There are huge catalogs of porn in every conceivable category. If you have seen any of it, it has shaped your expectations, whether you want it to or not.

Watching porn is a prevalent way people think they are learning about sex. Except porn isn't sex; it's entertainment. (It may be other things than that, too, but I'm not going to get into an evaluation of the value/health/morality of porn.) Not only is porn highly produced, with extensive preparation, enhancements, and selected camera angles, it is also based in fantasy and faking. These aren't, generally speaking, real people in real relationships and real situations. These scenes, looked at in the most generous way, are exaggerated to appeal to someone's eroticism, scripted to accentuate certain aspects of sex. They are a caricature of sex.

If porn is where you or your partner "learned" about sex, you're going to run into problems when sex meets real life. Certainly, what's shown in pornography is there for a reason; any slice of it is enjoyable for some segment of the population. But what porn presents is not how sex needs to be. Or how sex should be, unless it's exactly what you and your partner both want. Porn gives you one view of sex: it's not the only one. There are almost certainly things that you can learn about your erotic desires from watching pornography, but it is important to separate that insight from the expectations you have for sex with your partner. If you don't understand the difference between the fantasies being enacted in a photograph (or on screen) and the variety of ways sex can happen between two people in real life, you can end up with a distorted view of what sex is and what other people want. This informs your expectations, and you might view "regular sex" as inadequate or view yourself as inadequate if you can't perform like the porn stars.

Sexual myths spawn unrealistic expectations.

There are a lot of sexual myths in the world that create unrealistic expectations, too. I'm going to describe the myths that show up the most often in my work with couples. Some of this misinformation might have shown up while you were thinking about your family and cultural influences or considering how porn may have informed your view of sex. But whether they came up earlier or not, I want to correct the most common sexual myths that get in the way of good sex for couples (in no particular order):

YOU AND YOUR PARTNER SHOULD WANT TO HAVE THE SAME AMOUNT OF SEX.

The reality is that one of you is always more interested in sex than the other, at least over time (I will cover the topic of desire discrepancy extensively in Chapter 7). Which of you wants more sex and which wants less may switch, too, as life goes on. But a discrepancy in how much sex you want is not a problem. It can *become* one if you don't deal with it well, however. You can dispose of the idea that something is wrong just because one of you has a higher libido or interest in sex.

MEN WANT SEX MORE THAN WOMEN, AND THEY'RE ALWAYS READY TO GO.

In roughly half of the (heterosexual) couples I see in therapy, it's the woman who wants more sex than her partner. And in gay and lesbian couples, there is still one partner with a higher desire than the other. The sexual expectations that are based on gender can put a burden on you and your partner. If you're a man, you might feel a lot of pressure to be the sexual driver in the relationship—which can be very stressful if that's not how you feel. If you're a woman who wants sex, you may be judged for that, and at the same time, you might be judging your partner for wanting less. There is nothing about gender that determines what your sexual interest is or should be.

YOU SHOULD FEEL SPONTANEOUS DESIRE FOR SEX; YOU SHOULD FEEL "HORNY."

I describe two basic ways people experience sexual desire—proactive and reactive. Proactive desire is what people normally think of as libido or sex drive. If you have proactive desire, you feel desire for sex on a somewhat regular basis. You get horny, you think about sex, and you try to have it. You seek it out. You may think this is the right way to be, and something is wrong if you or your partner don't have this experience.

On the other hand, you may instead have *reactive* desire, a desire that needs to be evoked. You don't really think about sex. You may not get spontaneously aroused at all, or at least rarely. If you are asked if you want sex in any given moment, the answer is likely to be no. But your sexual interest is there if you go looking. If you enter a sexual situation, if you get kissed, touched, or stimulated, your body often responds. You start to get aroused. The engine turns over! You get turned on. And *then* you want sex. That reactive desire for sex (the desire that is sparked by a stimulus) is important. In my experience, about half of the population experiences reactive desire. And no, it's not all women! Some of you are like this from the beginning. Some of you switch in and out of reactive desire based on life circumstances. We all tend to move toward a more reactive desire as we get older. The bottom line is that your desire (and your partner's) is normal and valid.

Reactive desire isn't a problem. It's a valid way of experiencing sexual desire. But it requires the opportunity to arise. You must be willing to enter (or create) the encounter and see what happens.

No promises, no expectations, but be willing and open to getting turned on and wanting sex. And if you still experience no sexual arousal or desire at all, you and your partner will have to adapt to that, discovering ways to be sexual that still work for you and ways that you can find pleasure in physical touch.

SEX IS NATURAL; IT SHOULDN'T TAKE WORK.

Procreation is natural. Enough people have the urge to have sex that humankind hasn't died out yet. But the ability to have collaborative, creative sex with another person is a learned set of skills (skills I discuss in detail in Chapter 11). It isn't natural to be intimate or to share a meaningful experience. When you add in the complications of real life—kids, jobs, illness, and other stress—it makes perfect sense that your sex life is going to take work. It doesn't mean you're with the wrong person because sex isn't coming easily. You may need to let go of the fantasy that you can just show up and have good sex automatically. Even if it seemed easy early on when there was all that new relationship energy, over time everyone's sex life will need attention.

YOU AND YOUR PARTNER SHOULD KNOW WHAT THE OTHER WANTS; YOU SHOULDN'T HAVE TO COMMUNICATE.

This belief falls into what's called the "fusion fantasy" category—the idea that you will meet your soul mate, you will be perfectly attuned, and everything will be easy and natural because you found the right person. Unfortunately, this is a fantasy. It's perpetuated in popular culture, movies, and TV, which can make you feel like something must be wrong when it doesn't work out that way in real life.

Here is the truth: if you want something, you need to make that known, often with words. Yes, you can read each other and might have some good ideas about what the other wants, but often you don't have the required level of specificity. You do not instantly know how to please a partner. And what has worked with other lovers in the past won't necessarily work with you and your partner now. You are the only person who knows what your sexual activity feels like and how it could be better. It is up to you to give the gift of that information to your partner. They also need to give that to you. You don't have to talk through an entire sexual encounter, but you *will* have to communicate sometimes to get what you want.

WOMEN SHOULD ORGASM THROUGH VAGINAL PENETRATION ALONE.

Somewhere between 4-30% of women can or will orgasm only through the stimulation that happens during penetration. Most women require additional stimulation of their clitoris to reach an orgasm. You wouldn't know this by watching love scenes, however, since they rarely show anything but women appearing to climax through intercourse. If you are expecting a vaginal orgasm and you're not one of the rare women who experience that, you've set yourself up to feel like a failure. And if you're a partner who holds that expectation for your female lover, you may feel like at least one of you is inadequate.

If you or your partner are in a female body with a clitoris, you'll likely need to provide other stimulation, like fingering, oral sex, or a vibrator. And it will typically take longer than it does for a man to reach an orgasm.

MEN SHOULD LAST A LONG TIME.

This belief is about how long a man should be able to thrust in intercourse before having an orgasm. Again, what is portrayed in media and pornography would have you believe that men should be able to have sex indefinitely. The reality is most men will reach orgasm in two minutes or less of thrusting.

It is possible to develop at least some control over ejaculation, but that will likely involve slowing down or pacing to control the level of stimulation. It's also possible to learn to climax without ejaculation, allowing men to continue in sex and even have multiple orgasms, but that will take effort and dedication.

IF YOU ARE IN A GOOD SEXUAL RELATIONSHIP,
NEITHER OF YOU SHOULD MASTURBATE.

Apples and oranges. A lot of people with great sexual relationships still masturbate. First, there is always one of you who is more interested in sex, and solo sex is a great outlet for that extra sexual energy. Second, solo play is a different experience. It's less complicated. Sex with a partner involves teamwork, consideration of the experience for both people, more time, and more energy. There is nothing wrong with wanting a sexual experience with yourself, whether it's a quick, simple release or an extended, luxurious session of self-pleasure.

However, if you aren't in a good sexual relationship, as I suppose is likely the case if you're reading this book, you may be using masturbation to avoid your sexual issues. It's not that you shouldn't masturbate, but you shouldn't escape into your own experience at the expense of putting effort into your sex life with your partner. Ask yourself whether you are taking care of yourself so that you don't have to speak up to your partner about the state of your sex life. Pay attention to whether you avoid opportunities to connect with them sexually and then retreat into solo sex.

Your Takeaways

What did you discover about your sexual expectations? Do you see ways that they have been holding you back or setting you up for disappointment? Most of you have some assortment of mistaken and unhelpful beliefs. Recognizing them for what they are and deciding to let them go will be a crucial step in moving forward. It takes the pressure off, setting you on a course for success rather than a sense of failure. Loosening expectations lets you change how you think about sex, which is what I address in the next chapter.

CHAPTER 4

Change Your Mindset

Now that you have examined at least some of your expectations, it's time to take apart what it means to have sex and how you measure a "successful" encounter. I am asking you to set aside the beliefs and patterns that reinforce your sense of failure and disappointment. You're going to replace them with solid, helpful, and constructive beliefs and approaches that will be the foundation for positive change. It is time to take the pressure off yourself!

Before I move into a discussion of sex itself and how to improve your sex life with your partner, I need to talk about what sex is and what it's for. Unrealistic views of what constitutes sex are part of what causes people to avoid sex in the first place. So I want to define it for you now. Then I'll talk about how to *think* about sex so it's more approachable and how to *act* in the relationship so that you're more effective.

What is sex?

It seems like it should be simple to answer that question, but sex turns out to be quite difficult to define, at least in a way that makes it accessible to everyone. From my perspective, any definition of sex needs to be inclusive, include consent, be accessible for all bodies, and focus on pleasure and connection rather than specific acts or orgasm.

Consent is crucial. My definition of sex does not include anything that is non-consensual. Despite what is done with body parts, if it is forced or done under coercion or inappropriate use of power, like assault or molestation, that is not sex. When I think about what sex means and who can have it, I include every couple out there. If you are a couple adapting to life with sexual dysfunction that precludes intercourse, you can still have sex. If you are wheelchair bound and unable to experience sensation at all below the waist, you can still have sex. If you have different sexual anatomy, you can still have sex. It's all about finding whatever brings you physical pleasure and connection with your partner.

Look up "sex" on the internet, and you find several definitions: *sexual intercourse, especially between a man and a woman; sexual activity, including specifically sexual intercourse;* and, *any function or behavior involved with reproduction.* What? None of these definitions address pleasure and connection. None of them make sex accessible for everyone.

These definitions display what's called "heteronormativity"—where the assumption is that hetero is normal and everything else is, at best, an exception and at worst, a problem. Even if you are a heterosexual couple, "penis in vagina" as the definition of sex is still an incredibly limiting idea and isn't going to serve you, especially when you're struggling in your sex life. These definitions also demonstrate the ableism inherent in our culture—the discrimination in favor of able-bodied people. I hate these definitions, and I'm throwing them right out the window.

If you believe that sex is defined by doing certain things with certain body parts, you have set a trap for yourself. Because as soon as you either don't have the body parts or don't have the same use of those body parts, you are automatically failing. There is no reason think of sex that way, and there is every reason to loosen up your definition.

I want a definition of sex that is broad in its inclusion of actual behaviors, the capacities of differently abled bodies, and of all variations of gender, anatomy, and orientation, but I also want one that excludes (unchosen) acts of force and violence. My working definition is that sex is the physical expression of our innate drives for love, intimacy, and pleasure. Sex is about pleasure and connection—nothing more than that. And that can be easy. That can be fun.

I invite you to think about sex like you are going to the playground. You and your partner decide to head to the playground and figure out what to do once you're there. Nothing says you must go down the slide; maybe you'll just want to sit on the bench or swing a little bit. You get to decide as you go along about how you want to play together. It's the *outing* that counts, not the actual activities you engage in once you're there. If you can focus on playing together and not worry about the outcome, then you can enjoy your outing and sense of connection with each other. You will likely find that sometimes you end up more interested in sex than you would have predicted, simply because you got into it when the expectations were removed. Even if one person is more interested in sex than the other, there are different ways you can handle that—what I call "other endings." (I address these further in Chapter 11.) Because you have let go of the expectations, you succeed whenever you have pleasure and connection.

Adopt some new rules.

Now that I've defined sex in such a way that anyone can be successful, I have some basic directions, or "rules of the court," for the rest of this process. These rules are what I'd put in an instruction manual—if you were to get one when you enter a relationship. These rules of the court are fundamental to changing your mindset when it comes to sex and relationship, and they will be useful once you move into the action plan for improving your sex life.

And good news! While these guidelines are certainly applicable for sex itself, they can also apply outside the bedroom. These instructions can benefit your whole relationship from now on. They help build a good foundation for happiness with your partner.

YOU ARE RESPONSIBLE FOR YOURSELF.

Each of you is responsible for yourself. You are to play your own "side of the court" only. Play your side, and let your partner play theirs. It is not your job to take care of your partner, figure out what they're thinking, or make decisions on their behalf. That is their side of the court. I'm not saying you should be cruel or a brute or insensitive, but if you play your side well—you are honest, respectful, and clear—you should be able to trust that they will do the same. Part of playing your side is to say no when you need to say no (which I address in more detail shortly). You need to speak up about what you want and what you think and feel. You're the one taking care of you. If you each do that, the roles and responsibilities are clear. You develop a fundamental trust in each other to speak up and take care of yourselves, and that is essential for a good relationship and a good sex life.

YOU ARE RESPONSIBLE FOR YOUR OWN PLEASURE.

You are responsible for your own pleasure and your own orgasm (if desired). You may enlist the help of your partner, of course, but no one else owns your pleasure. That means, likewise, that you are not responsible for your partner's. You can be a willing participant, but it is not your burden to know what they want or to do it perfectly on your own.

SAY NO WHEN YOU NEED TO SAY NO.

When used properly, no is a good thing. You each need to trust that the other is taking care of themselves, so you can pursue what you want. If you can't trust their no, then you can't trust their yes. If your partner isn't safeguarding himself or herself, they will have sex they don't want, or they will engage reluctantly. In that case, you get a hollow experience or end up feeling like a villain who stole something. If your partner isn't saying no when they should, you'll either participate in unwanted sex and feel bad about it, or you'll start trying to read your partner and provide the no for them (perhaps by not initiating in the first place). Saying no is their side of the court. One of the clearest signs that they are taking care of their side is that they set boundaries when they need to. As hard as the word no may be to hear (or say), it can be a very good sign. Imagine greeting each no with "Okay, I understand. Thank you for taking care of yourself!"

Likewise, if you're the one who hasn't been saying no when you need to, you are undermining the trust in your relationship. This sets up your partner to either hang back or become tentative as they try to read you. Remember to take of yourself. Sometimes that means saying no. It may not be easy, but it eventually strengthens the foundation of trust and honesty.

Conversely, it is a problem when no is used to stonewall, and it can be hard to tell the difference. My basic rule of the court is to say no when you *need* to say no. When you just *want* to say no, it's time to evaluate your motives. Are you stonewalling? Are you holding out (or being stubborn) over some other issue? Can you stretch yourself out of your comfort zone and give them what they want and still feel good about it? Where is your no coming from? If it's stemming from something else that needs to be addressed, address it and move on. That way, when you're taking care of yourself, you can say "no, not now" more confidently.

WHAT YOU WANT IS OKAY.*

Each of you is entitled to want what you want. Resist any temptation to judge or villainize each other, whether it's for how much sex you want or don't want, or what kind of sex interests you. You need to validate your own desires, knowing that what you want is okay, even if you don't get a great reaction from your partner. Your wants may not match your partner's. The two of you will have to navigate the differences, but no one is wrong for what they want. I address this in lots of detail in Chapter 11.

OPEN IS BETTER THAN VULNERABLE.

Vulnerability is considered an asset and an aspiration by many people (speakers, writers, and clients alike), but I take issue with the current view of how important it is to be vulnerable. It may be semantics, but to me, vulnerable implies you can be decimated. I prefer the word "open." You can have the same authenticity, the same realness, honesty, and emotional availability and not be able to be destroyed by other people. You might get hurt, but you can have the strength and resiliency to be okay, learn, and move on. There is nothing good in being vulnerable, being so fragile that you're dependent on how others treat you to remain intact. When you feel vulnerable, you look to your partner to take care of you and make you feel safe. Instead, look at how you need to strengthen yourself to be okay so that you can remain open to your partner. They don't make things safe for you. You make it safe for yourself.

---

* There are a handful of exceptions that are illegal, non-consensual, and thus problematic. It's beyond the scope of this book to talk about peeping toms, flashers, frotteurism, pedophilia, bestiality, and such. I am talking about those desires that fall within legal and consensual bounds.

REAL SAFETY COMES FROM HONESTY.

Where your partner *does* contribute to your safety is with their honesty. A lot of people think that acceptance, softness, and warmth are what make you feel safe, that you are safest when your partner receives what you have to say with a smile and a hug. But you are not safe if that isn't how they actually feel. You are not safe if your partner can't or won't give you honest feedback. There is no safety if your partner turns a blind eye to your issues and their impact on your relationship. If your partner ignores his or her own frustrations and disappointments over time, you are not safe. Resentment will fester and grow, and it will come out eventually. At that point, you feel blindsided and your misplaced sense of safety comes crashing down.

Knowing that you will get the truth, no matter how painful it is to hear, creates a deep level of trust and safety. There is safety in being held accountable: hearing it straight from your partner about what they think, how they feel, and what they see in your behavior. In fact, this shows respect for you, demonstrating a belief in your ability to receive feedback and your interest in growth. And this way, you don't get surprised years down the road that your partner is unhappy. You also get the chance to fix things as you go along, preventing resentments from building up and escalating over time. This means more happiness together.

ASK FOR WHAT YOU WANT BUT TOLERATE NOT GETTING IT.

If you have a desire, speak up about it. Ask for what you want rather than not even trying, going about it passively, or trying to manipulate the situation. Use the words "I want" or "I would like," and then follow it up with a direct request about whether that thing can happen. For instance, you might say, "I would like to slow way down in sex and take more time before we have intercourse." This is a crucial relationship skill. And it's hard for a lot of people, especially if you learned as a kid that your wants didn't matter or if you were rewarded for not wanting much.

It is equally important that you can tolerate hearing no. Just because you muster the courage to ask for something doesn't mean you're going to get it. Your partner's desires matter, too. You will need to collaborate to create solutions that work for you both. My previous points underscore how important it is that your partner take care of themselves and that saying no can be a good thing. You're going to need to develop the strength to keep asking for what you want in life despite not always getting it.

IT IS YOUR JOB TO SHARE WHAT'S ON YOUR MIND.

As a rule, you should reveal what's going on in your head. It's not your partner's job to read your mind, notice you're upset, or drag stuff out of you. If you have something going on—a concern, a complaint, or something positive to share—you should bring it up with your partner. It's also your job to correct your partner if they are misreading you; share what you are really thinking or feeling.

This is different from how a lot of people operate. You may expect your partner to speak up when they notice you are sad or annoyed, thinking it's up to them to show openness to hearing from you. You may feel like they don't care about you if they aren't attuned to you and trying to figure out what's going on. Rather than expect them to read and pursue you, if you have something on your mind, share it directly. At least, you should do that most of the time. Knowing that you aren't perfect and may sometimes struggle to share your thoughts and feelings, there's some room for your partner to notice your demeanor and ask (and vice versa). But by and large, the burden is on you to bring things to the table.

LAY YOUR CARDS DOWN FIRST.

There's a common tactic of asking your partner a question to get a sense of where they stand on an issue before you reveal what you think. You can hide behind the question and play your hand from there, without revealing what you're thinking, feeling, or wanting. This technique can even be used to trap your partner: getting them to talk about something and then punishing them for whatever they say. My rule of the court is to play your cards first. Lay them on the table before you ask your partner to play theirs. Talk about what you're thinking or feeling and then follow it up with questions about what your partner thinks. This is intimacy—letting your partner see what's going on with you, being willing to risk their disapproval, and being able to stand by what you believe.

ALLOW YOURSELF TO BE SEEN.

The key to intimacy is letting yourself be seen, for better and for worse, for your assets and your faults. If you want true intimacy and look forward to enjoying your best sex life, you need to reveal yourself to your partner. You cannot hide or pretend and still expect to have great sex. People have non-intimate sex all the time, hiding who they are or putting up a pretense. It might be physically enjoyable. It may even be erotic (at least to one of the participants) since it allows you to create whatever meaning you want. But it doesn't create open and intimate sex—sex where you put yourself out there and allow your partner to see you. This intimacy, this revealing of yourself, allows you to pursue desire, reveal your preferences, be selfish in a good way, meet your partner's selfishness with gusto, and explore eroticism as a team. This is what opens the door to the best sex. Being able to show this much about yourself takes a solid sense of who you are.

Allowing yourself to be seen can be scary. It feels edgy to try something new, to share a new aspect of yourself, and to risk stepping into a deeper layer of your eroticism. That risk brings anxiety, and you will need an ability to tolerate that anxiety if your partner balks at your desires. Remember, you will not always get what you want, so it is important to be able to "hold onto yourself" and validate your own sexuality when your partner isn't receptive. The fear of a partner's reaction often keeps people from bringing their full selves to the bedroom. Encouraging each other to take these risks and to navigate new territory (whether it is novel sexual behaviors or adding eroticism to the sexual acts that are already on the menu) will enrich the sex you are having.

Find a way to meet your partner with curiosity, not judgment, when they let themselves be seen. And hold them accountable to do the same with you. Sometimes it will be hard to tolerate what you see in your partner (and what they see in you), and it's your job to figure out what to do about that. I talk more about exploring eroticism together in Chapter 11. But know that these explorations take a lot of communication and trust in yourself. You'll need to tolerate the anxiety of letting your partner see who you are and what you want as well as the anxiety you may have when you get a clear look at your partner.

EMPATHIZE FIRST, THEN RESPOND.

If someone is upset, empathize first. Hear what they're saying and make it clear that you understand it. Take the time to hear and understand them before you start constructing your response. You don't have to parrot it back or use elaborate communication tools, but you can make it clear that you really see why they are upset. That doesn't mean you agree with them, but you can see the situation through their eyes. Then you can proceed to converse about how you see it and how to handle the situation. By the way, this technique is valuable in all relationships, from parenting to work relationships to your life with your intimate partner.

ADDRESS THE "INTERPERSONAL GAP."

The Interpersonal Gap is the difference between what someone *intends* in communication and how it is *received* (as described by John L. Wallen in the 1960s). One of you says something with a certain intent; you're trying to communicate something to your partner. That message is affected by several factors. The lens and the language of you, the speaker, affect it. The message is impacted by the medium it flows through (think of trying to communicate in writing or over a bad phone connection). Additionally, it then filters through the lens of your partner. It hits your partner with a certain impact. If you or your partner has ever been triggered in conversation (reacting with a surprisingly strong emotional response), then you know how much your filter (or your past experiences) can affect communication. The difference between your intent as the speaker and the impact on your partner as the listener is the Interpersonal Gap.

To address that gap, you need to take apart what happened. First, if you notice the reaction doesn't match what you expected, that tells you there's a gap. Each of you should slow down and go through the message again. Get clearer about what your intent was in delivering the message. Figure out what filters or sore spots were hit and why. Hear from your partner about what the impact was. Follow up on this until you really understand each other and understand what went wrong in the communication. Do your best to give your partner the benefit of the doubt in these situations. Some of the earlier items on this list, like laying your cards down first and empathizing first, can help you do that.

YOU CAN READ YOUR PARTNER; ADMIT IT.

Your brain comes programmed with the capacity to read other people, to make a mental picture of another's mind (I highly recommend reading Dr. David Schnarch's book, *Brain Talk*, about this "mind mapping" process). This is a survival mechanism available in many species (all the way down to reptiles), meant to help us predict the behavior of another creature. You have elaborate and dedicated parts of your brain that read body language, tone of voice, facial expression, and more to allow you to understand the intent, feelings, and desires of another person.

You and your partner can read each other. You do it all day long, noticing changes in mood, understanding what each other wants, knowing how things are likely to affect each other. This isn't a problem. But it is problematic when you pretend you can't do it.

Returning to the example of exploring an Interpersonal Gap, you need to admit your ability to read each other. If you intended to be hurtful when communicating, your partner is going to know that. Don't hide behind the spoken words and pretend you "didn't mean it that way." This is a moment to be honest and own up to the fact that you did indeed want to hurt them (at least a little). Admit that you're mad or frustrated or hurt, and you want them to feel bad (or whatever is going on for you). You both know when you're doing it anyway. If the two of you start to own the darker sides of your motivations, you're going to have more respect for each other, as weird as that might sound. It takes a lot of integrity to be that honest.

VALIDATE YOURSELF RATHER THAN DEPEND ON VALIDATION FROM YOUR PARTNER.

You probably like the feeling of being accepted, approved, and welcomed by your partner for who you are, but it's a problem if you need it. That's when you start to hide parts of yourself, change into what the other wants, or pressure your partner to at least act like they accept you. The better strategy is to develop the strength to feel good about yourself regardless of how you are received by your partner. You should still be open to input, willing to consider the feedback you get from people who are important to you. But fundamentally, it's possible to know who you are and feel good about it, even if it doesn't make your partner happy.

As you take the steps toward self-validation, you will feel anxious. There is a transition as you switch to validating yourself, and it can leave you feeling alone and exposed. You'll have to sit in that anxiety and not do anything about it. Connect with yourself and what you know to be true about who you are. Confront yourself about your true motivations and deal with any parts of yourself that lack integrity. Once you know you are on solid ground, just stand there. That doesn't mean you never compromise or collaborate with your partner, but you can do that from a place of knowing who you are, what you believe, and that you can feel good about yourself. Practice giving yourself permission to be who you are and finding the feeling of being okay with yourself. You are in a much more stable and strong position once you decide you're okay than when you need acceptance from others to feel that way.

OVERCOME OBSTACLES.

Good sex is worth the effort it takes to grow into your ability to have it. Many of the ideas in this book require moving out of your comfort zone. Adopt an attitude of patience, perseverance, and lightness as you work to integrate these ideas into your sex life. Great sex takes time, maturity, experience, self-knowledge, and strength—qualities that take decades to fully develop and only come with practice. But it gets easier as you work on it. Each small step is huge and adds up to major change over time.

If you decide to try to implement some of my ideas (and I truly hope you do), whether in the touching exercise I will describe later in the book, or as a part of sexual encounters, you will find that they aren't all easy. You will get a good look at the challenges you face when you attempt to do some of these things. Don't be discouraged when some of this is hard. Running into difficulty provides good information. It prepares you to think about what you need to do and how far you must go to put these skills into practice. See this as an opportunity. Overcome the obstacles you will encounter. It requires a certain amount of patience, perseverance, and compassion for yourself and your partner.

Think of great sex as a lifelong pursuit. Your capacity for intense intimacy and personal connection will grow as you mature and develop as a person; it takes time. Be gentle with yourself and keep your goals of pleasure and connection in mind.

———

At this point in the book, you have a very clear picture of the cycle of avoidance and how painful it is to feel stuck and hopeless. You've recognized how your expectations drive your sense of disappointment. Hopefully, you're well on your way to accepting more realistic and helpful expectations so that you can feel successful in sex. You've also been exposed to new rules for relationship that make all this work easier. Now that you have this solid foundation for positive change, it's time to take the first action step. It's time to talk to your partner and get them on board.

SECTION 2:

DISCOVER THE ISSUES
AND YOUR ROLE IN THEM

CHAPTER 5

Honey, Can We Talk?

So far, this book has shown how people get stuck in a cycle of avoiding sex and why that happens. Now it's time to take the first step to escape that cycle by broaching the topic with your partner. This is where you're going to talk about the elephant in the room instead of skirting around it and pretending it isn't there.

It is possible for you to change your relationship just by changing your part in the dynamics. Two people can't keep doing the same dance if one person changes their steps. But it will be more effective if you do this with your partner; then you can co-create a new sexual relationship.

Perhaps you and your partner can talk easily about everything *but* sex, but it's also possible that you aren't yet skilled in talking about any of the hard stuff. You are certainly going to have trouble dealing with sexual concerns if you don't know how to navigate your disagreements in other areas of your life. It is crucial to be able to tackle difficult conversations, to disagree, and to tolerate anxiety and uncertainty. Lots of people tiptoe around each other, not knowing how to navigate the "eggshells." If you are afraid or unwilling to hurt your partner's feelings or to make them uncomfortable, you will keep important information to yourself. Do not swallow your concerns or bottle up emotions to avoid rocking the boat. Allow your partner to manage their own anxiety. Sure, you'll probably read their emotional state and wonder whether they can handle what you have to say. But say it either way.

Maybe you and your partner bring up the tough topics, but you end up bickering every time. One or both of you gets triggered. You shut down. Or you explode. You accuse and blame; or you beat yourself up. These emotional reactions that occur when you try to handle the hard things mean that you never get anything resolved. You may continue to try for a while, but it gets exhausting. And since it never solves anything, you start to avoid bringing the issues up.

Sexuality is one of our most primal, most core aspects of self. You are revealed when you share your sexuality with someone else, if you really let yourself be seen and exposed. If you struggle to handle difficult conversations about money, family, kids, work, chores, expectations, and more, I can almost guarantee that conversations about sex have been hard, too. Without a track record of solving hard problems together, you probably avoid bringing up sexual concerns, at least after a while.

It is difficult to talk constructively about your sex life when you're having problems. If it were that easy to dive in and talk about sex, the two of you would be doing it already. Part of what may have trapped you in the Avoidance Cycle is how hard it is to bring up the topic with your partner. But because you are reading this, it shows you are interested in changing your sex life. You want to be more than roommates, even if it is only because you know your partner isn't happy living this way. You already aren't having the relationship you want to be having, so I encourage you to dive in and bring your partner into the process. Once you can approach your sexual struggles as allies with the common goal of making your relationship better, you can proceed through the book, using the conversations and exercises laid out here to help improve your intimate relationship.

If you and your partner haven't been talking about sex, much less having it, someone needs to speak up first. It's going to take a little courage to bring it up. It will almost certainly be scary, but there is no other way to start. There will never be a perfect time, so stop waiting for the right moment. Rip off the Band-Aid! There are decent odds that your partner isn't happy, either, even if they've been silent on the subject. Ask your partner if the two of you can talk. You can begin by laying it on the table: you are concerned about your sex life. Bring up the fact that, as a couple, you have been avoiding the topic of sex and that you want to work on making your relationship better.

It certainly helps to ground the conversation in the hope for a better relationship, sexual and otherwise. Talk about how much your relationship matters and how much you want it to thrive. Express your willingness to own your part of the problems and your desire to focus on moving forward. There might be difficult issues that need to be addressed, but it can still be done with a focus on the positive improvements you want to see.

Do not simply blame your partner or expect them to talk about how they're feeling right away. Adhering to the idea that you should play your cards first (as described as one of my rules of the court in Chapter 4), it's best to start by revealing what's been going on for you. Here are some questions to first consider asking yourself, in order to share the answers with your partner:

- How have you been feeling about your sex life?

- What are your contributions to the sexual issues?

- Where have you been avoiding intimacy?

- How have you deflected or ignored their attempts to have sex or to talk about it?

- How have you done a poor job of seeking understanding of your partner's perspective?

The more you can lead with your own self-confrontation, the better the conversation will go. On the other hand, don't allow your partner to hide behind that and just blame you. Each of you needs to take responsibility for your own part of the equation if things are to improve. What follows is a list of skills and examples that will help you form these conversations and make these talks easier and more productive.

Differentiate between feelings and thoughts.

Discriminating between thoughts and feelings can be especially difficult, but this distinction is important if you want to stay grounded and want your partner to participate in the work. I encourage people to differentiate between:

- what has happened (what a video camera would show)
- the thoughts you have about it (what meaning have you attributed to what happened)
- how you feel about it (what emotions have been triggered)
- and what you want (your request)

Let me give you an example. You might say, "I feel like you don't value the contribution I make to the family," but this is not a *feeling* statement. (Feelings fall into one of four basic categories: sad, mad, glad or afraid.) You probably *feel* sad and resentful, but you *think* your partner does not appreciate you and you *think* they don't value what you do. This distinction defuses the tension because acknowledging that you have added your own meaning to the feelings underscores that they are just your *thoughts*; they are not absolute or even necessarily correct.

Use "I" language.

Use "I" language as much as possible, describing your own experience and your reaction to it, without making it about the other person. Don't label or judge your partner. Don't be attached to the idea that what you think and feel is right. Your feelings are valid because you are having them, but that doesn't mean they're accurate. Recognize and own that you are making meaning out of events; this keeps your conversation in the realm of exploring what's happening for *you* instead of attacking your partner.

So, let me return to the example of "feeling like your partner doesn't value your contributions to the family." A better way to say that might be: "I realize I feel sad and resentful about how much I think I do for the family. I have this story that you don't even notice all my effort. Or that you don't care or value the ways I contribute. This belief keeps me distant from you, and I can tell it's really in the way of our relationship. Will you explore with me what I'm thinking and feeling so we can move it out of the way?"

Confront yourself first.

Start by facing yourself honestly. Admit your negative parts and acknowledge their role in the situation. If you feel stingy or greedy or jealous or resentful, say that out loud and own that this is your stuff to deal with. This demonstrates that you are willing to admit your faults, and it sets the stage for your partner to do the same. For example, to return to the case of not feeling like your partner appreciates your contribution, you might say, "Now that we're talking about it, I know I have a part of me that is a martyr. I do a lot around the house that you don't even expect. I take more on that I can handle, and I struggle to ask for help. Sometimes, I don't even tell you I've done something. I wait for you to notice, and then I end up getting resentful when you don't. I have been too afraid to bring this up and address it, and that's on me. Going forward, I am not going to secretly pick up the slack, and I am going to talk to you to work out a more equitable way to share the responsibilities."

Make a request but remain flexible.

Ask for what you want without expecting that you will get it. It is important to advocate for yourself and talk about your desires. But your partner is a different person with different and equally valid desires. Make room for the validity of your partner's experience, too, and consider his or her wants as you offer your own.

Anticipate pushback.

Making sure you keep the subject on the table is even more important than bringing it up in the first place. Be prepared for some pushback or procrastination from your partner as you start talking about improving your sex life. If you are serious about tackling the topic, your partner will read that in you. They will either step up and engage with you, or they'll dig in harder and refuse to address it. Your determination matters. No matter what response you get from your partner, make it clear that you're not willing to ignore it anymore.

As you are talking about your disappointing sex life, keep in mind that at least one of you probably feels sad, believing they are broken or inadequate. The root cause of avoidance of sex is unmet expectations. Something hasn't been going well, and avoidance has become the way to deal with it. As you move into the next steps of improving your sex life, give yourselves permission to get rid of all expectations about what sex should be. Talk to your partner about changing the mindset about sex, as I discussed in Chapter 4. Embrace the new rules of the court together so that you can take pressure off the process. Understand that any sexual dysfunction you are dealing with might change what you can experience in sex, at least in the short term, and let that be okay. Figure out what's possible for now and learn to enjoy that. Freedom from expectation means you can be free to play again. Once you're reconnecting in your sex life, sex often becomes easier and some of the problems might disappear. And in fact, once you have addressed your role in the sexual issues, you'll likely find that your other relationship issues get better, too. Improvements in sex ripple out to the rest of your relationship.

If you and your partner are now in agreement about improving things together, you can move into the conversations that are going to form the "discovery" part of the process. If you are still doing this on your own, you'll have to explore the topics by yourself. If you and your partner are not in agreement, it will be even more important to push forward and act unilaterally to change your relationship and the dynamics around sex. The goal of this section is to get clear about your own, individual contribution to the cycle, so you will be prepared to change your part. The first place to look for information about your role is in your personal history, in what's colloquially called "your baggage."

CHAPTER 6

Who Packed Your Bags?

This is where you start to figure out what you are bringing to the dynamic with your partner. Every situation in your relationship is co-created by you and your partner, and your problematic sex life is no exception. One reason you may not have dealt honestly with your sex life until now stems from your own patterns of dealing with difficult things. Your specific contribution to the cycle, the way you participate in this cycle, is not a coincidence. You have your challenges for a reason (and they likely show up in more than just your sex life).

When beginning to explore where your patterns were developed, you can start with what's called your family of origin—your childhood. While it's not "all about your mother," as Freud might have said, it's worth looking back over your childhood and getting real about how things were and how your personality developed in that context, with all the important people in your life at that time.

I'm going to ask you to think about and answer a whole host of questions that shed light on your patterns and where they originate. It may be helpful to use a journal to record your responses. Hopefully you will gain some clarity about how you were trained to behave and react to things. Go through these with your partner and share your reflections with each other (or answer them yourself if you're doing this on your own). Take as much time as you need, and let the conversations go where they may. My questions are starting points and prompts, but I want you to really dive in and understand your background and that of your partner. You might want to have separate conversations about each of the topics below.

Look at your family history.

The process starts by examining your nuclear family—you, your parents, and any siblings. Your childhood home and the people in it will have had a strong impact on your beliefs, expectations, behaviors, and coping mechanisms. Take your time discussing the following questions with each other or reflecting on them on your own:

- What were each of your parents like, if you knew them? How was your relationship with each of them then, and what's it like now?

- What type of relationship did your parents have with each other, if they had one?

- Are they still together? If not, what do you know about their separation, divorce, death or other reason for not being together?

- Who are your siblings? What are they like? What is your relationship like with them now and how was it when you were young?

- What roles did you each have in the family growing up? How are those the same or different now?

Go over the same kinds of questions for stepparents, stepsiblings, and any important extended family members.

POWER IN YOUR FAMILY

After discussing the members of your nuclear family, it is important to think about how your family handled power. Every family will come up with some way of deciding who is in control of various aspects of family life. There is an inherent power differential between adults and children, but it can show up in a variety of ways from one family to the next. For example, some kids are "parentified" (given more power than they should have). In other households, adults abuse the power they have, and kids have little to no control. Power can be wielded more subtly, too, but even that would have shaped your development growing up.

When talking about family power dynamics, you should also examine the power between the adults in your childhood (parents, grandparents, stepparents, aunts and uncles, godparents—anyone you might have witnessed in power struggles during your formative years). Spend some time with the following questions:

- Who made decisions? Who got their way and how?

- Did the people in the family acknowledge who really wielded the power? Or was there a way of pretending things were different than they were?

- How was power handled among the adults in your family? Between adults and children?

- Was power ever misused or abused? How? Did you push back?

- How much power did you have growing up? How did you feel about it?

- How did you know where you had power and where you didn't?

- What was your take away about power? How do you tend to handle power dynamics in your life now?

LOVE AND SUPPORT

Families differ in whether (and how) they show love and affection. Some of you will have been raised feeling loved and supported; others will have known from the beginning that you were on your own. Your family environment shapes your attachment style and expectations in relationships throughout your lives. Experiences with physical touch, emotional support, and reliability have a direct impact on romantic relationships as an adult. What do you learn when you explore the following:

• What did affection, love, and support look like in your family (if there was any)? Who was it between? Where didn't it exist?

• Who would comfort you after a hard day at school?

• On whom did you rely?

• What kind of support and love did you see between your parents, if any?

• In what ways have these experiences shaped your tendencies with love and affection as an adult?

SEX

Your family has a big impact on your attitude toward sex. Some of you come from families that were open about sex, talking about it and treating it as a healthy part of life. Some of you got only a little, if any at all, exposure to the topic of sex. Sex was a taboo subject or just absent from any conversation. And others of you grew up in an environment where sex was explicitly negative, either from the way people talked about it or because of how it was acted out or used in the household. Reflect on these questions to explore how your upbringing has affected how you feel and think about sex:

- Did your family talk about sex? In what kind of way?

- Did you get "the talk?" Who sat you down and how did that go? What were the messages you got?

- Was there any sexual energy between your parents? How did you feel about that? Was it appropriate and within bounds? Was it excessive and lacking boundaries?

- Was there any sexual energy between anyone else in the family? Any sexual contact? What happened? Was it known or acknowledged by family members? If so, how was it treated? How did you feel about it?

- Did you have any experiences where you were discovered in sexual activity? What happened and how did the person react? How did you feel?

- How has your family environment and attitude about sex affected you? What impact does it have on your sexual relationships as an adult?

CONFLICT

Your family and upbringing teach you about dealing with conflict. Many of you come from homes where keeping the peace was important. You learned not to need anything and not to rock the boat. Others may have come from chaotic environments where conflict was a constant presence—perhaps even a threatening reality. Many of you were raised with something in between: conflict existed, but you didn't necessarily learn to deal with it well (in a way that would be satisfying to all parties and lead to mutual understanding). To have a strong relationship with your partner, it's important to learn about your comfort level with conflict as well as your skill set for handling conflict with others. Consider the following prompts as you evaluate what you learned about conflict:

- How did your family handle conflict? What behaviors did your parents exhibit during disagreements?

- Did conflict get resolved in your family? Or did it fester and come out as passive aggressiveness?

- Was conflict scary in any way? What happened that made it so?

- Were you allowed to disagree with adults as a child? How did you get that message?

- What about conflict between you and your siblings? How did that go? What did your parents do about it?

- What was your basic takeaway about conflict? What are your tendencies now when it comes to addressing or avoiding conflict?

SUBSTANCE ABUSE AND MENTAL ILLNESS

Many families struggle with the complicating factors of mental illness or substance abuse, and these will usually have dramatic effects on family life and relationships. Besides the impact of the disease itself and how each family member is affected by the problem, there are family dynamics around admitting and addressing the issues versus avoiding and pretending that they don't exist. Discuss the following questions:

- Were there substance abuse issues in your family?

- If so, who struggled? How were they handled?

- How did the household adapt to the use?

- What about mental illness? Were any of your family members anxious or depressed?

- Did someone struggle with a more significant disorder?

- How did these struggles play out in your house as you grew up?

- What was your role around each of those topics? How did it change the way your family members related?

- Was your family open and honest about any challenges? Did they pretend in public? Did they pretend at home?

- What did you learn? Are there issues with substance use or mental health that are relevant to your life now?

SECRETS

There can certainly be secrets about any of the topics covered so far. Families often act like nothing is wrong amid problems, even very serious ones. Your family may have taught you to turn a blind eye on problems or that appearances matter so much that you can't acknowledge problems. Secrets may have been used to manipulate you, to put you in positions of power or powerlessness. You may have been encouraged to keep secrets or to break them. All of this has an impact on whether you deal with things directly or whether you prefer to hide. Explore how secrecy played out in your family:

- Were there secrets in your family? How do you know? What were you told and what did you infer?

- Were there money issues? Were these spoken about? How did the family navigate around the topic?

- Was there infidelity? By whom? How do you know or come to suspect? How did your various family members treat that?

- Were there other things left unspoken?

- What were you expected to do? What did you do?

- What did you learn about honesty versus secrecy? How do you handle secrecy now?

- What are your tendencies toward dealing openly with issues versus hiding them?

In talking about your family and its experience with love, power, conflict, secrets, substance abuse, mental illness, and more, you can probably see how you ended up with the baggage that you have. Most of your baggage was packed for you; you didn't get to choose your experiences, your training, or your beliefs.

Regardless of what type of home you were raised in, you were raised in a way that gave you messages about how you should behave and what's expected of you—and what you learned is not the same as everyone else. Your experience (and theirs) is unique and impactful.

Growing up, you learn what earns you praise, what gets you punished, and how to be left alone. If you have never examined this before, it can be hard to see it at first—it's like the water you swim in—but you grew up in different water from other families. It's common to assume everyone grew up with the same influences, but it's important to realize that your family was unique, and in fact, your experience is different than those of any siblings you have, too. There is nothing absolute about how things need to be *now*, in your relationships as an adult. You need to see that your patterns are adaptations to your environment—and recognize you can change them, too. You don't have to keep everything that is packed in your baggage!

Examine your sexual history.

Now that you have examined your family life and how that shaped your personality and coping mechanisms, it is time to look back at your relationship and sexual history. It's not only your family who has put things into your baggage. You need to understand your sexual beliefs and expectations when you're trying to improve your sex life. Again, go through these topics and questions with your partner (if they are working with you) or alone (if not). Take all the time you need and see where the prompts lead.

ABOUT SEX

Think back to the messages you received about sex—in your family, your culture, your religion, your community, and from media and other sources. Think about what you learned about sex as you reflect on the following questions:

- What things were said to you about sex and intimacy?

- Where did those messages come from? Family? Church? Friends? Other places?

- What messages were unspoken?

- How much of what you heard seemed relevant to you?

- What parts of it were shaming?

- How were you viewing sex by the time you entered adolescence? Did you think it was the best thing since sliced bread? Shameful, dirty, and wrong? Scary and unknown?

- What expectations about sex have you developed?

- How do these messages and views impact you and your sex life now?

YOUR SEXUAL IDENTITY

Your sense of yourself as a sexual person develops over time. Some of you have always had a clear understanding of who you are and what your sexual interests are. Others may still be struggling to figure that out. You have a personal journey in getting clear about your sexual orientation, gender identity, and sense of your eroticism. Your path may have been direct and short, or it may have taken a more roundabout route. Learn more about the unfolding of your identity by discussing these prompts:

- What was it like for you as you became aware of yourself as a sexual person?

- What did you know about your sexual orientation and gender? How did you feel about it?

- How has your understanding of yourself changed over time?

- How did you come to understand these aspects of yourself?

- How did you feel about your body? How do you feel about it now?

- What issues arose around you figuring out how you identify in terms of gender and orientation?

- How were you supported, or not, as you learned about who you are?

- How has this exploration shaped your experience of sex and your expectations of what it can be?

- How might you feel limited or affected by your identity?

EARLY SEXUAL EXPERIENCES

Your past sexual experiences inform your expectations and desires, one way or another. Perhaps you rebel against the things that have happened to you, determined to live differently in the future. Or perhaps you absorbed your experiences, and they dictate what you come to expect in a relationship. For some, early experiences were positive. But for others, they were disappointing, shaming, scary, or confusing. It's worth understanding and sharing what your experiences have been and how they have affected you. Go through these questions and see what you learn:

- What were your earliest sexual experiences?

- How did you feel about them at the time? How do you feel about them now?

- Do you wish you had had more sexual experiences? Fewer?

- Did you self-pleasure? How did you feel about it?

- What messages did you get about that?

- What about chosen experiences with other people?

- How did these experiences shape your attitudes, beliefs, and expectations about sex? How are they relevant to your current situation?

Sexual trauma

So many people have had traumatic, coercive, confusing, or inappropriate experiences with sex and sexuality in their history. This can have a profound effect on future sex lives. Depending on whether you have had these experiences *and* whether you have processed and dealt with them, you may need additional support in moving forward in your sex life. There are therapists that specialize in working with trauma, and there are resources available for the process. If you think you are still highly reactive or triggered around sex, if you find yourself upset or dissociated during sex, or if you have never talked to anyone about your experiences, I suggest you seek out that extra support. I have listed some books that could be helpful in the resources section at the end of the book. When sharing answers to these questions, tread gently. Feel free to take care of yourself if any of this material is triggering to you or your partner. Take your time with the following exploration:

- Did you have experiences that were not chosen or were exploitative? What happened?

- What did you understand about it at the time? How did you feel about it? How do you view it now?

- Do you blame yourself for what happened? Do you feel bad about how you handled it or how it felt to you, good or bad?

- Did you tell anyone? Were you believed, supported, and protected?

- Were you shamed, scolded, or blamed?

- What sense did you make of it?

- How do you think these experiences have shaped your view of sex? Your expectations? Your ability to enjoy sex with your partner(s) since then?

Previous relationships

It is important to look back over your significant relationships, if you've had any before your current one. There are usually patterns that emerge both about who you pick and how you show up in relationships. Apply some focused thought to these questions:

- What have your partners been like?

- What drew you to them?

- What kinds of things happened in those relationships? How did they end?

- How did you feel over the course of those relationships—in the beginning, in the middle, in the end?

- How did they treat you? How did you treat them?

- How was the sex? What happened in your sex life with other partners over time?

- Do you see some patterns? What information emerges that might shed light on your current dynamics with your partner?

Working in therapy, I cover family, relationship, and sexual history with everyone, because everyone has a story that shapes who they are in relationships. Through your exploration of all this personal history, you have learned a lot about who packed your baggage and what's in it. You've learned what's influenced you in how you handle love, sex, power, conflict, and more. You probably have some clear ideas about what your patterns are and how they impact your relationship now.

Your Takeaways

Your job, moving forward, is to be responsible for what you're going to do about these patterns. I want you to have a list of specific ways you contribute to your situation and then have an idea of what it would look like to do things differently. Some of this will take experimentation, and some of it just means doing the opposite of what you typically do. This is your work—changing your patterns that aren't serving your relationship now.

Consider all the conversations and reflection you've done so far. What is your tendency in relationships—to pursue or to distance? What is your role in conflict—either during it or in the avoidance of it? Do you keep secrets? How do you perpetuate the role you had in your family? What's your relationship to power? What are your expectations of a partner? Of sex? How has your sexual history shaped you? What else do you see that might need to change?

———

Now that you have looked back into the past to understand its influence on you today, it's time to take a hard look at your present situation. You are going to examine additional reasons why you may be avoiding your sex life—and why it makes sense that you do.

CHAPTER 7

What Are You Avoiding?

There are some very good reasons you are avoiding sex. There are real issues you face that are making sex difficult or disappointing. In fact, so many things can affect sex that it's almost inevitable that you would struggle at some point. This chapter is about finding out what the issues are that impede your sex life with your partner. As before, I want you to think about how you are handling these issues and what you need to do differently to improve the situation. You will then pull all of this together and focus specifically on your role in the dynamic and address this in an upcoming chapter.

Consider sexual desire issues and the desire discrepancy.

Issues around sexual desire are a very common reason you might be feeling bad about sex. If one or both of you has a hard time wanting to have sex, not only are you less interested in it, but you also run up against the expectation (from yourself, your partner, the world, or all the above) that you *should* want it. Once it seems like something should be different than it is, you can get self-conscious, self-critical, and avoidant. It's difficult to engage in something that makes you feel inadequate.

When someone's libido drops (either yours or your partner's) or seems low, that person struggles to feel desire for sex. Worry over this state of affairs (by both parties) makes it even more difficult to get interested. As you get older, your desire often becomes more reactive, as well, as I discussed in Chapter 3. You don't feel horny or think about sex in the same way or as often as you used to; now you need stimulation and mental engagement to be interested in sex. These changes mean it's harder to be interested enough to take the time and trouble to get in the mood. When sex becomes hard work, it's no wonder you struggle.

Desire discrepancy (when one partner wants sex more than the other) between the two of you is another thing that can throw your sex life for a loop. There is always one partner who wants sex more than the other, at least over time. You might change roles—in different relationships or over time—but one of you is going to be the person with more interest in sex. This isn't a problem by itself, but it can become one when you get caught in the traps of a desire mismatch. I will describe the traps here, and I will discuss what to do about them in Chapter 9.

DESIRE DISCREPANCY TRAP: FOR THE PERSON WITH MORE DESIRE

If you're the person with higher desire caught in the trap, you typically feel rejected. You want sex, and you take your partner's lower level of desire personally. If the other person doesn't want sex, it must mean you aren't attractive, desirable, lovable, or important. At that point, sex begins to take on extra meaning—proof that you're all those things or confirmation that you're not. In fact, you may feel an increasing urgency to prove these and to reassure yourself, generating even more of a focus on sex. You may come off as controlling, with frequent sexual initiation, pressure, and not taking no for an answer.

You, as the person who wants more sex, can also feel controlled. The person who wants sex less, due only to that fact, ends up in control of sex. They get to say if, when, and how you have sex, and it starts to feel like you're left to accept whatever crumbs the other is willing to throw you. You get resentful. You're not happy about this, but you may be willing to take what there is since you don't know when your next chance for sexual experience will be.

It's common for the person with more desire to do most of the initiating. You may bring up your interest in sex frequently, trying to get something to change, and end up fighting about it. Those conversations probably go in circles. Or maybe you've gone quiet hoping that your partner will notice and pick up the slack. Maybe you've stopped talking about it, resigning yourself to feeling unfulfilled and unhappy. You give up on trying to make a difference in your sex life. Perhaps you alternate between these ways of handling it.

Likely, you feel like something is wrong with your partner because they don't want sex. Where is their natural sex drive? Is something broken so they don't feel what they're supposed to feel? Should they go to therapy and figure this out? You might feel more sexually evolved or open and want to help your partner let go, open up, or grow sexually. It's also possible to assume something is wrong with your level of desire, that you want it too much, or that you put too much importance on it.

DESIRE DISCREPANCY TRAP: FOR THE PERSON WITH LESS DESIRE

If you're the partner with less desire who is caught in the trap, you feel pressure. You are always mindful that your partner wants sex, and you are aware that they're unhappy. Their interest in sex can feel like a constant presence in the room, never letting you relax. You can't imagine having the time or space to cultivate your own interest in sex. When faced with the possibility of sex, you weigh how long it's been since the last time you did it against how much you don't really want to have sex. This can lead to giving in, when you don't think you can get away with saying no again.

Perhaps you get annoyed with your partner for their level of interest in sex. It can feel like they just want sex, not you. Your position is always in response to your partner—yes or no to their desire, yes or no to their suggestions, yes or no to the pressure you're feeling.

It is likely you have some very good reasons for not wanting the sex that is offered. You may know how good sex can be or have a sense of your wants and desires but think (or know) your partner can't handle that or isn't interested. As you watch your partner accept the poor level of sex you're having, you're losing respect for them even though you're the one offering them crumbs. Yet you don't take the risk to speak up or take responsibility for your own sexuality.

Since you seem to be missing this drive that others seem to have, it may also feel like something is wrong with you, that you are inadequate or broken. It may be that you haven't found or explored what makes sex engaging for you, and so it seems like your sex drive is missing.

DESIRE DISCREPANCY TRAP: BOTH OF YOU

Regardless of what side of the trap you are in, you probably pathologize each other to some degree—regarding or treating each other as abnormal or unhealthy. You may criticize your partner's level of desire. If you're the one who wants more sex, you may have been accused of only thinking about sex, always wanting sex, or maybe even of being a sex addict. If you want it less, you may be labeled as repressed, frigid, withholding, or broken—implying that something is wrong since you don't have what's considered a "normal" sex drive.

Consider performance issues.

Some of what you consider your "performance issues" may just be your experiences not living up to your expectations. You think you have a problem because you can't last a long time, or you don't orgasm through penetrative sex. Those feelings of inadequacy are based on misguided information. Other "dysfunctions" stem from the presence of something that turns you off in the sex you are having. Sometimes you really do have sexual dysfunction that haunts your encounters. If you are embarrassed or ashamed of this, you're likely to avoid sex. If your partner reacts badly to your difficulties in sexual functioning, that makes sex even harder.

It's important to deal with any issues you're having with sexual function. Seeing a doctor is an important first step, although you may need persistence to find someone who's ready to help and not just suggest a pill or a glass of wine (though sometimes those are exactly what's needed). Especially in cases of sexual pain, you'll need to find an experienced professional. You may also want to work with a certified sex therapist to help as you change what you can change and adapt to what you can't. If you confront the issues you're having directly, you're likely going to find less need to avoid sex. Even if you have a chronic or permanent change to your sexual functioning, you can adapt together if you have the right foundation of information, support, and an open attitude about what sex can be.

Consider issues of loss.

There are losses in life that can affect your sex life, whether related directly to sex or not. When sex confronts you with the reality of what you have lost, you may start to avoid it because it's emotionally painful. Your losses need to be grieved and processed so you can take the steps to approach your sex life with joy again.

I highly recommend Edy Nathan's book, *It's Grief*, as a resource in your process.

LOSS WITH ILLNESS AND DISABILITY

Loss becomes a stark reality with the diagnosis and experience of a chronic illness or disability. If you are struggling with heart disease, cancer, diabetes, HIV/AIDS, mental illness, or physical illness or impairment, you face a variety of losses, and many of them relate to the expression of your sexuality. The way you thought about your body and yourself as a sexual person can change when you become sick or disabled, affecting your identity. If you can no longer have sex the way you used to, you have lost your familiar sexual interactions and the sensations you were accustomed to. If you have lost body parts or the use of any of them, your body may no longer feel comfortable or familiar, and some sexual behaviors may now be out of reach. These are all losses that must be accepted and grieved before you can move on to create a new chapter in your sexual life.

LOSS WITH SEXUAL TRAUMA

If you have been sexually molested, abused, or assaulted, you have suffered loss. Not only do you deal with the emotional and physical trauma of your experience, but you may feel robbed of your innocence, your ability to trust in people, your opportunity to relax and enjoy sex, and your willingness and eagerness to express yourself sexually. Sex can become a very loaded topic—tolerated and avoided or indulged in risky and excessive ways. Again, grieving the losses and treating the trauma become part of the path to reclaiming a healthy sexuality for yourself.

LOSS WITH CHANGES IN SEXUAL FUNCTIONING

You also deal with significant loss if your body stops responding sexually the way you want it to. Whether due to aging, relationship issues, or psychological reasons, you may find your body is difficult to arouse, slow (or too quick) to orgasm, or that you are easily distracted. These physical changes in functioning can also result in changes to your confidence, body image, and sexual self-image.

LOSS AROUND PREGNANCY AND CHILDBEARING

Infertility and miscarriage can create a tremendous sense of loss that arises during sex. If you are a heterosexual couple longing for a baby, that sense of loss is present with you every time you engage in the act that you hoped would create one. If you are a woman trying to get pregnant, you may grieve every time you get your period. If the sex you have isn't the type that would create a child, you can still face the sadness of the longing for a family in those most intimate moments. It takes time to process that grief and fully enjoy life again.

THE LOSS WITH DISCONNECTION FROM YOUR PARTNER

You may feel a profound sense of loss if you are sexually or emotionally distant from your partner. What promised to be a rich celebration of love and intimacy can dry up, leaving a hole in its place. Relationships that started with a robust sex life can creep slowly into the sexual desert, in which sex is rare, routine, disconnected, or nonexistent. You may experience this as a significant loss, although the sadness and loneliness can be hidden behind resentment and anger. When you do have sex, you may still encounter the sadness that your sex life or relationship isn't working well overall.

Consider relationship issues.

If you have problems in your relationship, eventually that's going to show up in the bedroom. And if you're avoiding those problems, you'll also likely end up avoiding sex. The same parts of you that struggle to deal with things directly in your relationship are going to make it hard for you to deal with your sexual issues. For instance, you may want to avoid hurting your partner's feelings at all costs. You may be uncomfortable with confrontation or challenge. You may hide parts of yourself that would have to come out if you were going to really address the problems. You and your partner may have communication issues that keep you from working well together and feeling close.

A lot of relationship issues can improve by working through this book because they require the same skills and personal growth you're going to develop as you address your sexual concerns. However, you may find that you have more serious issues that need to be addressed first, before you are able to work successfully together to improve your sex life. It's going to be difficult, if not impossible, to be allies in this work if you and your partner experience cruelty, major power struggles, controlling behavior, substance abuse, or violence. If that's happening, you'll need to be honest about what's going on, own your part, and confront the issues that cause resentment, anger, and emotional escalation. A good therapist can be instrumental in that process if you and your partner have been stuck in negative patterns for a while.

Consider lack of knowledge and experience.

Having an accurate frame of reference about sex helps you set realistic expectations and have confidence that your experience is normal and healthy. When you are suffering from a lack of knowledge or a lack of experience, it's easy to doubt yourself.

A lot of people don't have much knowledge about sex. In some ways, our culture leaves it up to us to reinvent the wheel and learn sex on our own. So how do you learn it? Mostly with other inexperienced people trying to figure it out, too. You make your way through sexual experiences, having some you like and some you don't, but not necessarily equipping yourself with the tools you need to have an impact on whether sex gets better for you or not. If you and your partner can talk about what's happening in sex and what you like and don't like, you're better prepared to craft a sex life that works for you. But if you struggle with communicating about sex, growth is less likely to happen. And if you haven't had much sexual experience, then you haven't had the chance to figure out what you want or how to get it.

Sex education isn't much help. If you had it, it was likely focused on preventing teenage pregnancy and scaring you using pictures and descriptions of diseases. There are basic anatomy lessons and some instruction about insertion, but that's the scope of the lesson on how to have sex. And that only applies to heterosexual couples with the expected anatomy and functioning, leaving out a huge segment of the population who are left feeling like they are out in the fringes of sexual experience and relegated to the extra chapter in every book. Some of you have read some great books about sex, I'm sure, but may not have had the chance to put it into practice. And you will find that even if you have the book knowledge, it's a whole different thing to get it all working with an actual person.

Examine sex negativity and shame.

Feelings and beliefs that sex is bad and shameful may very well get in the way of you enjoying a fulfilling sex life. If you were raised in a culture that either didn't talk about sex or explicitly talked about it as bad, dirty, sinful or scary, it may be hard to shake that training. It can be difficult to embrace your sexuality and the joys of sexual expression.

If your family or social culture taught you that sex is negative, you may have a hard time even recognizing those messages. Your beliefs will show up in your behavior and your feelings, and you may have to work to uncover what they are and where they come from. As you discovered in Chapter 6 when looking at your own history, it's hard to see the water you swim in. You tend to assume that what you learned growing up must be true. If you were taught sex negativity through your religious background, you may be in an even a bigger bind. It may feel like a violation, sin, or breaking of faith to question your beliefs or to pursue certain sexual behaviors. (You may want to seek out the book by Tina Sellers listed in the resources section.) You will need patience and support as you take apart your beliefs and decide for yourself (and with your partner) what your limits will be.

Look at issues due to aging.

As you get older, your body changes. You know this, but it will probably still surprise and upset you when it starts to happen. When those changes show up in your sex life, it can be especially upsetting.

One common change is that you need more stimulation in order to reach the same level of arousal. As Dr. David Schnarch describes in his work, you need a certain amount of stimulation (a combination of physical and mental) to get physically aroused (to get lubricated or erect), and then you need a higher level of stimulation to reach an orgasm. You can think of these as thresholds—like a bar you need to get over to physically respond the way you want to. As you get older, those bars get higher. You need more stimulation to achieve the same result you got more easily when you were younger.

In addition, you may have other changes that occur with age. Women (here I am talking about female-bodied people with a vagina, uterus, ovaries, and vulva) generally go through menopause, during and after which it can become more difficult to lubricate, and there can be some discomfort or pain with sex. Some women will report libido changes. Vaginal tissue often gets thinner and more prone to damage. Not all women experience the same changes, but it's common to experience at least some change in one of these ways.

Men's bodies change with age, too (here I am talking about male bodied people with a penis and testicles). Erectile dysfunction gets more common and tends to get worse with other medical conditions, too. Libido can drop. The refractory period (how long it takes to be able to have sex again) generally gets longer.

Even if you don't have the anatomy referred to above or don't experience the changes described, there are other effects of aging that will impact your sex life. You tend toward a bit more pain in your body, less range of motion in your joints, and lowering stamina. Age brings medical problems that can have sexual repercussions. Certain necessary medications have sexual side effects. All of this can have an impact on your sex life.

If you and your partner are experiencing age-related changes in your sex life, this may be a reason you've been more prone to avoid sex. It's hard to feel like you are meeting sexual expectations when your body is functioning differently than it used to.

Children have an impact.

Research shows that marital satisfaction drops with the arrival of children, and it doesn't go up again significantly until after they leave the house. Maybe if someone told you this ahead of time, you'd rethink your decision to have kids! As much as they can be a joy and the light of our lives, having children often affects the relationship and sex life between partners.

If you have young children, you know that privacy, free time, and energy are in short supply. The needs of the kids seem ever-present and (mostly) of highest priority. It's common to put your marriage on the back burner—even if you didn't mean to. Some couples use a tag-team model, where you trade off the kids, so one can get some other things done, leaving minimal time for you to connect as a couple. Parenting can cause some serious issues between partners, too, and cause more discord and tension than in the past.

As the kids get a little older you may have more time to yourselves, but the parenting challenges often get bigger. You may be dealing with some serious behavioral or other issues with your older children. If nothing else, parents are often swamped with activities, carpooling, and sporting events.

If your sex life is being impacted by the fact that you have children, you've got to factor that into your understanding of what's happening (or not) in the bedroom.

Consider any trauma you or your partner have experienced.

I wrote about trauma when I asked you to reflect on your sexual history. Trauma, whether it's "Big T" or "small t" trauma, can have an impact on your sex life. If you or your partner find yourself emotionally triggered by sex or by certain activities, it is hard to be present and engaged in your body. These triggers make it difficult to relax and trust. You may struggle to know what you like or to get aroused. If you've had some sort of trauma, and it is affecting your sex life, you need to allow extra time and space to work through the trauma and its emotional effects. Again, consider a therapist or specialist to help you move past it, but at the very least you need to be gentle with yourself and work as a team with your partner as you reclaim your sexuality. It's important to understand what your triggers are so you can work to defuse them (where possible), and work around them (if necessary).

Consider the impacts of illness and disability.

If either of you has a disease, especially a chronic condition, it is likely to impact your sex life. Some illnesses have specific sexual side effects. Heart disease and diabetes can both affect your ability to get physically aroused. Some medical treatments and medications create sexual side effects. Plenty of diseases just make you feel lousy: affecting your energy level, your ability to be present, and your interest in being sexual at all. If your condition is temporary, you may be able to just wait it out. But if either of you is dealing with something chronic or long term, you'll have to find a way to adapt your sex life to accommodate the condition.

If one of you is disabled, that will likely have an impact on your sexual functioning. You'll have to consider exactly what is different for you—in terms of sensation and movement—and determine what is available to compensate for this difference. The human body has an incredible way of compensating for losses, so use the whole body when exploring what's pleasurable and possible. If you focus on pleasure and connection with your partner, you'll find ways to share a sexual experience together.

Examine body image issues.

A lot of people struggle with body image issues or self-consciousness in sex. Being "in your head," criticizing your body, or wanting to hide, means you are not present in the experience with your partner. You are probably far removed from the pleasure you could be having. If one of you has gained weight or had some other change while you've been together, that person may be especially self-conscious about their body now. Worrying about your body is a common reason to avoid being sexual. On the one hand, you can certainly start to do what it takes to move toward the body you want to have. On the other hand, there's good reason to make peace with who you are and accept yourself now, so you can live your life and enjoy yourself without always waiting for the day when your body looks like you think it should. I share resources for addressing body image issues at the end of the book.

Sexual aversion can be a problem.

Some people avoid sex because of an aversion to bodily fluids or a belief that sex is just gross. Often people are also bothered by other bodily functions and situations. It takes some work to overcome these reactions. You can certainly see a therapist to help you, or you can try a basic exposure desensitization approach, working your way to comfort with parts of the body and their secretions. You can only sanitize sex so much, but you can start with clean bodies, towels nearby, condoms or latex barriers, and a dose of patience.

Gender issues can affect your sex life.

Sometimes people avoid sex because their gender is not straightforward, and they don't feel comfortable in their body. This can be because you don't identify with/as your assigned gender, which can make using some body parts confusing or unpleasant. Even if you chose surgery to change your anatomy, you may have a complicated relationship with your new body, needing to learn to accept it and how to find and give pleasure in this new form.

Other people struggle with gender because they are not clearly male or female. There are almost two dozen different medical or genetic conditions that fall in the spectrum of "intersex" that mean someone does not clearly fit into a binary view of gender. For some of you, this was discovered at birth, and you may have been assigned a gender or surgically altered as an infant or child. For others of you, the condition was only discovered later, as a teen or adult. Without fitting into a clear category of male or female, and perhaps without having the genitalia you might expect, you may experience confusion, embarrassment, shame, or self-doubt when you have sex. You may have to expand what it means to have sex. Find a way to be open with your partner about how you feel and what's going on, so you can work together to make sex enjoyable.

Medical and surgical changes need to be considered.

If you've had surgery to change your body, especially your sexual parts, you will likely have to adapt to the new you. Whether that surgery has been to change or adapt your gender, or the result of medical treatment (like mastectomy or prostate surgery), your body is different, and your sexual functioning may be affected. Your core sense of yourself as a sexual being may have changed. If these changes are positive, if they bring you into alignment with who you are, you may have an easier transition, but it's still going to take time to feel at home in your new skin and adapt to your body in sex.

If those changes are negative or unwanted, the result of an accident or medical treatment, you likely have loss and grief to deal with on top of learning to have sex in your new body. These are complex changes and can easily lead to avoiding sex. Talking openly with your partner is crucial. They are likely timid about bringing this up and may struggle to know how to talk about it. If you can open the topic and share what's on your mind, it makes space to hear how the changes have affected them, as well.

Your Takeaways

There are a lot of different issues that can complicate your sex life. You have considered many of the common influences that can make your intimate life even more challenging than it would be otherwise. Get clear about which of these factors are at play in your life. Do you have children? Is age, illness, or disability having an impact? Has one or have both of you experienced trauma? Issues with body image or gender? Surgery? Are there losses that impede your sex life? Are there relationship issues that get in the way of your ability to want to have sex? Do you struggle with sexual desire? Are you caught in the traps of a desire discrepancy? What else is making your sex life more difficult?

———

Phew, that's a lot! Are you feeling overwhelmed at all the information and discovery in this chapter? There are so many ways sex can get difficult, and all these reasons make sense. Some of you have more baggage than others, but hopefully you've gotten a good look at the various influences that are making your sex life more difficult than it needs to be. Don't worry; even if there's a lot to unpack and discard, you can lighten your load.

Now that you have a good understanding of the kinds of issues that contribute to your problems, it is time to look at your unique dance around sex. You will take apart both how you have and how you *don't* have sex to understand how these ideas come together to sabotage your sex life.

CHAPTER 8

What Is Your Unique Dance?

At this point in the process, you have inventoried the problems that make it natural for you to avoid sex. Now it's time to look at how sex itself is working (and not) under your circumstances. Even if you are the only one reading this book, if you change *your* thought process, behaviors, reactions, and expectations, your sex life will naturally have to change. Sex will gradually become easier.

Consider what I term the "dance" around sex. I use the word dance because so much of what happens between couples is non-verbal. Examine what you and your partner *do* when you have sex and when you don't, and you'll discover there's almost a choreography to your interactions.

What does it look like when sex is hard? In this chapter, I will walk you through a series of questions—like those you'd answer if you were in therapy—to discover your steps in the dance. Notice that many of my questions ask you to reflect on what you're reading in your partner. As I have already established, this information is a big part of what's happening between you. It's time to talk about that openly. You will end up with your sexual encounters laid out in front of you like a movie. Watch what's going on and recognize everything that each of you is doing and why. Uncover your choreography.

Who initiates sex and how?

The first thing to look at is your pattern around initiating, or not initiating, sex. Couples who are struggling with sex often end up with one person doing most of the initiation, in whatever form that takes. Looking at how and when that is done, with all the subtle signals you read in each other, is part of the process of acknowledging what you both know is unspoken. Consider both the verbal requests as well as the physical bids for sex that one or both of you make. Go through these questions as a couple and discuss each one:

- Which of you will typically initiate sex? How?

- Does one of you initiate considerably more than the other?

- Is the sexual initiation verbal or physical? What exactly happens in this situation? Does the other person recognize it?

- If you're the one initiating, or at least used to be, what made you decide to do it then? What makes you back off and not suggest it?

- How much are you "reading the room" to make your decision, and what do you see that makes you approach or avoid sexual initiation with your partner?

- What signals do you throw out to keep your partner away or to invite them in?

- How are the two of you communicating about what you want and don't want without words?

- Do you acknowledge what's happening or let it go without addressing it?

- If one of you is avoiding sex, how are you accomplishing that? How are you disguising that avoidance?

How do you talk about sex?

Next, let's address how you both communicate about sex at this point in your relationship. It's probably difficult for the two of you to honestly talk about your sex life now that sex itself has become difficult. You may have been avoiding this conversation for a long time and have some well-worn techniques for keeping it at bay. I want you to go through these questions and be as real as possible about how you have handled the topic of the sexual issues in your relationship. You're hurting yourself the most if you hold back or hide. Apply some focused thought to these questions:

- What happens when one of you tries to talk about sex? Who does that and how? When? How often?

- Do you have a conversation about it or find a way to deflect? How is it deflected?

- Does one of you bring up something unrelated to divert the talk? Does the other person persist or allow themselves to be diverted?

- If you do talk about your sex life, are you being real and honest about what's happening? Do you blame your partner? Do you blame it on other circumstances in your life?

- Are you being direct about your thoughts and feelings or holding them back because you're afraid to tell your partner?

- When your partner is talking to you, how much are you willing to accept a cover story or a surface explanation? Are you afraid to hear them say the truth?

- Do you both collude to keep the conversation on relatively safe ground?

What happens during sex itself?

Let's take apart what happens in sex when you have it. Most long-term couples, struggling or not, develop a basic way they usually have sex. I want you to talk about what sex looks like for you now, at this point. Slow it down and go through the details; that will help you see how you read each other and how you proceed with what you are reading. Directly examining your sex life may not be pretty. In fact, it probably won't be since you're struggling with sex. That's okay; it's why you are here. Just get it all out now and know you'll be working to make it better very soon. Again, several more important questions to help you:

- When do you know you're moving toward sex instead of avoiding it?

- What is the signal that you give that you're willing? Or what do you read in your partner that tells you it's a yes rather than a no?

- What are you thinking and feeling at that point in time?

- Where are you in your head? What's the story you have about what's happening?

- And what do you think is going on for your partner?

- How does sex proceed? What happens next? And next?

- Who is in charge of the pacing? Who is reading the scene and deciding it's time for each next step?

- Are you talking to each other during sex? Is either of you saying what you like (or don't)? Are you arguing during sex? Are you talking about extraneous things, like the kids' carpool?

- What are you thinking and feeling?

- How much are you reading what's happening for your partner and using that to judge what should happen next?

- Is any of this overt or is it all unspoken?

- If sex is a problem, at what point does it seem to go badly? How do you know?

- What do you do in that problematic moment? What does your partner do?

- Are you talking about it?

- Does everything come to a screeching halt or do you change directions?

What happens after (and between) sex?

When sex is a struggle, you may have more of an aftermath than an afterglow. Sometimes there can be peace and joy when it's gone well (or if it's happened at all), but many times you and your partner may end up frustrated, disappointed, sad, confused, or upset. That can then feed your avoidance cycle. Look at what you do after sex is over, both immediately and between sexual encounters:

- After sex, how are you feeling?

- How do you think your partner is feeling?

- What do you both do once it's over?

- How do you know it's over?

- How does the cycle of avoidance show up for you two? How do you avoid talking about sex? How do you avoid having sex the next time? Why?

- What exactly is your role in the cycle?

- What will you admit if you are willing to get honest about what you're doing?

Your Takeaways

Pay attention to your steps in the dance. Look at where you are being direct and where you're being evasive or misleading. Notice how you influence what happens and where you try to control what your partner does. Consider how your actions are interpreted by and affect your partner. What are some things you could change about your contribution right away? What became clear in this evaluation about how sex gets off the rails for you? What immediate ideas do you have about how it could get better?

——

These series of questions deconstruct your sex life and shine a light onto what's happening under the surface. There is usually a whole dance around sex that is largely non-verbal and unacknowledged—even though both people are aware of what's going on. When I have these talks with clients, it's clear how much both people understand what's happening even if they never talk about it. Which is why you should talk about it!

Slowing it down and admitting what you both already know allows you to talk about what's happening with some compassion and curiosity. While it can be difficult to be honest about some of these dynamics, it takes a bit of the pressure off because you don't have to pretend anymore. You are now informed and armed to transform your sex life. Hopefully, after tackling these lists of questions, you have several ideas about where the problems are and what has kept you from addressing them. You should have several concrete ideas about how your own issues and behavior are making things worse. The next step in the process is to get clear about your contribution to the problems.

CHAPTER 9

What's on Your Side of the Court?

So far, this book has provided opportunity to consider a variety of issues that might be at play in your own sexual struggles. While it makes sense that these contributing factors would make it harder to have and enjoy sex, that doesn't mean you have to let them keep you stuck. Now is the time to reach clarity on how they are affecting *you* and what *you* are going to do about it.

As you move forward in this process, only play your side of the court. I've mentioned that concept before, but now it is time to come up with concrete ways you intend to change your role in your sexual difficulties. You do your work, and your partner does theirs. You can hold each other accountable, to a degree, but do not worry about them or police their efforts. Do everything you can to solve your own part of the problem. To be successful, you need to get clear about exactly what your work is.

Handle your desire discrepancy.

If desire discrepancy is part of the problem between you and your partner, take on your half of that and deal with it in a healthy, constructive way. I use a concept developed by Dr. David Schnarch and suggest that you consider your role in the dynamic from two different perspectives: where is your best self in charge, and where is your worst self running the show?

The best in you is the part that is honest. It's the part that can settle your own emotional state and manage your reactivity. It's the part that can connect with what you want and communicate that. The best part also keeps you safe by knowing you're going to be okay. In a way (maybe surprisingly), it's the part that could choose to leave the relationship if your fundamental bottom lines aren't met—at least after a good, solid effort with your partner.

YOUR "JOB" IF YOU WANT LESS SEX THAN YOUR PARTNER

Let's look at what's happening if you're the person with less interest in sex. We've already talked about how the person with less desire controls sex. Your partner wants sex more, so you're the one saying yes or no, when and how. If desire discrepancy has been a problem in your relationship, then your partner has likely derived their sense of desirability and self-esteem from your sexual response, allowing you to control their sense of adequacy. You may or may not welcome that power.

The best in you is showing up if you don't want to have sex just to bolster your partner's ego. It can be good judgment to be repelled by overtures for sex that come from neediness or obligation. The best in you knows you want a shared sexual experience that is about pleasure and connection, not validation. Your best self knows what good sex is (or can be), or you don't know, but you are willing to figure it out for yourself. The best in you recognizes if your partner's higher level of desire isn't based in a developed ability to really connect in sex, to share moments of intensity, and to be present with you. So you may be showing good sense in not wanting the kind of sex you've been having with your partner. There may be other ways that the sex you're having is subpar or problematic, giving you good reason not to want it.

And your best self may also be standing your ground about how much sex you're willing to have.

While some of your lower desire may be solid and coming from a good place, because you object to the sex itself or the meaning it has, you still need to challenge yourself about the parts of your motivation that aren't coming from your best self. Do you enjoy the power you have and wielding it over your partner? Perhaps you enjoy the pain it's causing them because you have your own resentments that you don't deal with directly. Putting off your partner and focusing on their issues is a way of not addressing your own anxiety or limitations. Your partner's issues can be used as a diversion, even if they're real, so that you don't have to deal with your own. Don't force your partner to carry the emotional brunt of your withering sex life. Sit down at the table, figuratively, and craft a solution. This is the time to stop waiting for just the right invitation and to begin stating your needs (or even acknowledging that you have any). The worst in you may think you're perfectly happy sitting in your comfort zone, unwilling to stretch while knowing full well that your partner is suffering. The best in you is not.

The key is to figure out what's happening and confront yourself about it. Where the best in you is in charge, where it makes sense for you not to want sex, you need to speak up and do something about what's wrong instead of avoid sex. It's not fully from the best in you if you won't talk about it, address the issues, and work toward solving the problem between you. Where the worst of you is showing up, you need to take it on. While you can get benefit from communicating with your partner and taking a stand, it is your job to challenge yourself to act differently. It is your job to take a more active role in solving your sex life. It is time to clean your side of the court. That will entail stepping up, determining what it takes to want to engage in sex, and designing a real contribution to a sex life that works for both of you.

If you're the person with the higher level of desire, you've got the same two basic questions—what part of your role is from the best part of you and what part is from the worst?

The best in you is showing up when you advocate for what you want—knowing that sex is important to you and valuing it. Speaking up about what matters and not just letting it go is important. The best in you shows up when you're in touch with what you like and what turns you on. If you've figured out your desires, preferences, and eroticism, you've gotten in touch with core elements of yourself. If you validate those desires, too, giving yourself permission to want what you want instead of needing your partner to make them okay, that is a sign you're coming from a solid place.

The worst part of you shows up when you rely on validation from your partner to feel good about yourself. You take their lack of sexual interest personally, as rejection. Your sense of yourself—as a person, as a lover, as a partner—requires their sexual interest. When you have sex, you feel good about yourself and your relationship. But without sex, you get shaky. Sex is reassurance. This changes the meaning of sex from connecting with your partner to making you feel okay about yourself. This is usually unpalatable to your partner, who can tell this is a form of neediness, and then they become less interested in sex.

The worst in you is involved, too, if you believe (or pretend to believe) you are sexually evolved and enlightened while your partner is repressed or inadequate. If your conversation never gets to why your partner legitimately isn't interested in sex and how it might not be fulfilling to them, you're not challenging your pretenses. You can have lots of interest in sex but still plenty of issues around intimacy. You may struggle to get emotionally close to your partner, able to be physical in sex but not open in other settings or in other ways. Maybe you can be sexual when someone doesn't mean as much to you, but you struggle if your partner matters to you. Your libido can be a smokescreen for your own challenge with having a true connection with your partner.

The worst in you is in charge when you have whatever sex is offered to you, abandoning your own desires, preferences, and eroticism to keep the peace. You take whatever scraps you can get. This suggests to your partner that you have no taste, that you can't discern good sex from bad, and you just want to get off. You are feeding a cycle that undermines your partner's respect for you, and probably eats away at your self-respect, too.

Dealing with your half of the desire discrepancy is going to require taking yourself on and behaving differently. Speak up about the things you know to be a problem and where you know you are on solid ground. Claim the validity of your desires and continue to advocate for yourself and what you want. But also confront yourself about how you've needed your partner to respond a certain way for you to feel good about yourself. Admit when you've been willing to blame your partner without looking at your own role. Get honest about how you are challenged to show up, be seen, and have true moments of connection. Figure out the ways this situation is about you and your own limitations instead of blaming or pathologizing your partner. Decide what you're going to change in your interactions, so those changes originate from your best self.

Master your own emotional regulation.

Self-soothing and emotional self-regulation are big parts of the work for each of you. Develop the ability to tolerate anxiety as well as feeling unsettled and unsure. Instead of looking to your partner to change what they're doing or to reassure you, settle yourself down and tend to your own reactivity. This is going to take practice, but playing your side of the court means regulating your own emotional state. You can take a break to get control of yourself, but then it's your job to show up and engage again. If you get triggered or escalated, it's your job to notice that and do what you need to do to regain control. It's also your job to let your partner take a break when needed and not hold them in discussion against their will. It's your job not to call names or blame your partner. Avoid taking the bait or throwing fuel on the fire. Each of you has that job, but your side is the only one that you need to focus on.

Adjust your expectations.

Another part of playing your side of the court is adjusting your expectations. Recognize your own expectations and how those have shaped your interactions with your partners. Where you have unrealistic notions about sex, acknowledge and change them. This requires letting go of things you might have thought were important and accepting a new view of how relationships work. There may be some sense of loss and a need to grieve some of these ideas. It's hard to let go of the idea that someone who loves you should just know what you want. Or that sex should be easy and not need any work or effort. The idea that you and your partner should orgasm at the same time, through penetration, or repeatedly is based on unrealistic expectations. But keeping expectations like these sets you up to fail, feeding the cycle of avoidance you are trying to change.

Give your partner the benefit of the doubt.

Find ways to extend the benefit of the doubt to your partner. You may be coming into this process with a lot of bad history and hard feelings, but without forgetting that, be willing to see this as a fresh start. Focus on what you must do and allow your partner the space and responsibility to tend to their own work. Don't worry yet about how they are doing, and don't jump to conclusions that they aren't doing what they need to. A lot of this work is internal, so you may not see anything right away. That doesn't mean they aren't changing. Focus on you, not them. Assume the best instead of the worst, especially if they make a mistake. Unilaterally giving your partner the benefit of the doubt and honestly assessing what happens is a big part of getting into a virtuous cycle instead of a vicious one.

Be honest.

Perhaps the hardest part of playing your side of the court is the need to be completely honest. You may think you're an honest person, but the true test comes when there's a lot at stake. You need to be honest even when it's going to cost you, even when it might cost you the relationship and when it really isn't what your partner wants to hear. Unless you're telling the truth and coming clean when it's risky, you're not an honest person.

Real trust is based on this kind of honesty, as I described in Chapter 4. Your partner cannot trust you if you hold back to spare their feelings or "make them safe." They will not trust you if you swallow your feelings and concerns only to blindside them later. Trust will not exist if you neglect your own needs and wants, building resentment over time, even if you are doing it to keep the peace or be accommodating.

You also need to be honest about your ability to read your partner and how you use the information you get when you do. Most people are not avoiding sex by being direct and overt; they do it by sending signals to their partner and by reading the signals sent in return. It becomes collusion between partners, a covert agreement enacted by two people. Once you begin talking about your interactions, including the fact that you are sending and reading signals, you start to deal with the real issues.

For now, having this conversation can be scary. One or both of you have invested in the pretense that you can't read the other. You may fear what's going to be revealed about you or your relationship if you honestly open up. Once you get honest, you can't go back to pretending you don't know. There is no unringing that bell—and that is a good thing, although it feels risky.

There isn't room anymore for pretending. Don't mislead your partner about what you're thinking or wanting. Don't hide behind half-truths or deflection. Don't avoid telling the truth or sharing what's going on for you by focusing on your partner and their issues. You and your partner read each other; it's time to admit it and deal directly with what you know about each other.

Your Takeaways

This is the part of the process where you gather steam to make change, getting clear about what your role is in the problem. You have taken a good look at your thoughts and behaviors, and you have examined several ways that people typically struggle to do their best in relationship. Tie this all together and make it personal. What do you need to do differently to manage the difference in sexual desire with your partner? Where do you need to improve in your ability to manage your emotions with your partner? Where does anxiety take over and keep you from doing your best? You've already explored a lot of your unrealistic expectations when you examined your history; which ones do you need to change? What can you do that allows a fresh start? How can you contribute to a virtuous cycle with your partner? What do you need to get honest about? Where have you been hiding and pretending you don't know what's happening between you?

———

Every relationship, every dynamic, and every interaction are co-created. But you can only analyze and change your part. Yes, your partner's behavior has an impact on you. You may need to bring up what they're doing and how that is affecting you. But focus on changing the parts you can control, the parts that are about you. You and your partner are on the same team in this process. You are allies. Doing your part as a teammate means taking this seriously and acting unilaterally, whether or not your partner is doing the same. This is a commitment you make for yourself: to do your work and to clean up your part. Every time you encounter a difficulty or are tempted to focus on your partner and their mistakes, confront yourself first. What part is yours? What could you have done better? What were you really thinking and wanting? Is there something you could do that would change the outcome and more reliably lead to what you were trying to accomplish? How are you not being honest or direct? Answer these questions, then confront your partner in a respectful way. Holding someone else accountable is a respectful thing to do; it shows you think they can do better. Part of playing your side will be (respectfully) calling out your partner, but that only comes after you've taken a good look at yourself. Most of your effort at this point needs to be focused on your own contributions. Now get excited. It is time to move on to the stage where you transform your sex life.

Before you do, let's revisit the example couples to see what they learned through this part of the process. Each person has examined their family history, their sexual and relationship history, and their sexual dynamic with their partner. Each has put together these pieces and gotten ideas of what they need to work on individually. They have a strategy for moving forward, knowing what they want to change and transform.

Carol and Todd

Carol and Todd are the older couple nearing retirement.
Carol is a breast cancer survivor,
and Todd is experiencing erectile dysfunction.

Carol:

Carol was raised in a conservative family that never discussed sex. It was a taboo subject. With her limited information, she formed a view of sex that is narrow and rigid: sex equals intercourse, and anything else is dirty. Although she and Todd enjoyed a relatively active sex life for years, they didn't talk much about sex, and they never made any effort to shake it up or challenge their comfort levels. Now that they face sexual challenges, she has a hard time being open and creative about sex. She also realizes her sexual experience is very limited. She has had only one other sexual partner, and the sex in that relationship was also focused on her partner's pleasure and on intercourse as the goal. She's had a lifetime of knowing one way to have sex and no preparation for what to do when that doesn't work.

She needs to adjust her understanding about what sex is, and she needs to accept that sexual function and responsiveness change with age. She must challenge her view that sex equals intercourse. She also needs to sever the connection she has created between *her* desirability and *his* sexual arousal.

Their situation also exposes how uncomfortable she is with his penis; she didn't need to tackle her squeamishness in their earlier sex life because Todd was easily aroused. She must change her expectations about what Todd needs and what her role is in providing it.

Lastly, she is only now seeing what a significant impact her mastectomy has had on her sense of self and her sexuality. By avoiding sex in recent years, she avoided facing how big the changes and challenges are for her. She needs to grieve the losses associated with her cancer, and then she needs to find ways that she can enjoy her body again. She must find a way to let herself be scared and nervous with Todd as they explore sex together.

Todd:

Todd's family was open about sex growing up, so he didn't come into their marriage with a ton of baggage about that, but his family did not handle conflict well. Everything was about appearances, so no one addressed their concerns or frustrations with each other. He was trained to suppress his feelings, to put his head in the sand, and to avoid talking about what was obviously happening around him. Everything would seem fine on the surface, but he could tell that things were festering underneath, especially between his parents. That was proved true when his mom left the home suddenly, when Todd was 13. She moved in and out of the household a few times during his teenage years, and he did not see her often when she wasn't living with the family. No one addressed it directly, and his dad would mostly act like nothing was happening. He always thought he was fine with this situation. But now that he is reflecting on it, he is getting in touch with how painful it was not to understand the events and how much he missed his mom. He realizes now that he is driven by the fear of losing relationships. It keeps him from rocking the boat. As a result, he doesn't know how to handle difficult conversations.

Todd sees that he has rigid expectations about sex, too. He's been focused on penetrative sex as the only goal, so he is thrown for a loop now that intercourse is a struggle. He feels "less of a man" when he can't get or maintain an erection, and that has shaken his confidence. It wasn't so bad when he just needed some stimulation to get erect, but now that he needs a pill (and that doesn't always work), he feels inadequate. He needs to change his definition of successful sex as much as Carol does. Todd needs to put effort into being less goal-oriented in sex and expand what he finds pleasurable.

Todd also sees that he wasn't raised to share intimacy with people he loves. No one discussed or shared feelings, and there was no openness between family members. He knows he hasn't been open about his feelings with Carol, either. He has an inner world (thoughts, feelings, and beliefs) that he has never talked about. He has felt closer to her over the years when they shared experiences together, including sex, but he recognizes that he never explicitly made that clear to her. He hasn't talked to her, before now, about how sad and inadequate he feels. He hasn't been willing to tell her how important she is to him. He needs to let her in and let her see how he thinks and feels about things.

In addition to sharing the "nice" feelings, he's got to learn to speak up and to take a stand about the things that matter to him. He must risk having the hard conversations required if he is going to get what he wants. He needs to work through (or tolerate) his fear of losing people, so he can take up some space in the relationship and give himself room to get his needs and wants met.

Beth and Yara

Beth and Yara are the couple in their 40s, married, and who fight about other things without addressing sex. Beth struggles to get aroused, and Yara is feeling more sexually awake. They struggle with desire discrepancy.

Yara:

Yara is the only daughter in a family from a male-dominated culture. Throughout her life she has been expected to be simultaneously attractive and yet pure. She absorbed a sexual shame, from both her culture and her religion, about sex in general and specifically about her own sexuality. She's confused about what's okay—in sex, in relationships, and in her sexual desires. Her opinions haven't mattered in her family. She was expected to take care of her mom's feelings, to keep Mom happy and stable. Because her mother was rageful and controlling, Yara has grown up believing that she failed and is bad. She grew up walking on eggshells around her family, and she finds herself having the same reactions around Beth. As an adult, she still feels bad and guilty when anything is wrong in her relationship. She needs to overcome the shame she feels about sex, as well as her tendency to assume that she is wrong. She needs to validate her own desires and speak up about what she wants.

Yara is also very uncomfortable hurting Beth's feelings. Her family role was to be the good girl and make everyone happy. It's almost intolerable to have someone she loves displeased with her. This has her trapped; she can't get in touch with what she wants for herself, and she sure can't say anything about it if it might rock the boat. She realizes she'll have to learn to speak up and tolerate the anxiety she feels if Beth is unhappy. She also needs to confront Beth about judging her for her sexual preferences.

Beth:

Beth's childhood home was chaotic; her role in the family was to make sure things kept running, helping her sister get to school and even cooking many dinners as she grew older. Her parents had traditional roles based on gender. Beth's dad had the power in the family. Her mom both chafed at that, being critical and petty, while also using it to avoid grownup responsibilities by relying on Dad. Beth never saw a partnership of equals when she was growing up.

Beth's mom was angry and controlling, somewhat like Yara's. Beth's dad cheated on her mom repeatedly when Beth was young. Her mom made no effort to hide her jealousy and rage about this. Beth has absorbed a fear of abandonment from both her parents' relationship and from her own benign neglect as a child.

Looking at her own behavior now, Beth realizes she is more like her mom than she wants to admit. Her jealousy and anger dominate the household with Yara. She feels a lot of anxiety about Yara's flirtatiousness and her sexual energy with men. She's been controlling Yara's activities and friendships, and she hasn't hesitated to make Yara feel bad for doing things without her. She feels inadequate and insecure, and that keeps her from being able to address her fears constructively. She needs to change her behavior and tolerate the distress arising from her own self-doubt. She needs to talk honestly with Yara about what she's feeling, and she needs to develop the ability to regulate her own emotions, without insisting Yara be the one to make her feel better.

Beth's relationship history is a string of committed partnerships with women. She always considered herself a sexual person, and she generally believed herself to be both sexually open and skilled as a lover. The shift in her sexual desire and responsiveness at this point has completely undermined the confidence she once possessed. Beth can see how much she has projected her own sense of sexual inadequacy onto Yara. She needs to admit what she's been doing—pushing Yara away by making her feel bad so that Beth herself won't be in an uncomfortable position. After allowing herself to grieve how her body has changed, she needs to give herself the space to explore how her body works now. Importantly, Beth also needs to learn to quiet her mind and be present.

Jenny and Rich

Jenny and Rich are the married couple in their 30s with two young kids. Jenny has no desire for sex and has stopped having sex out of obligation, which she'd been doing for years. Rich feels rejected and hopeless.

Jenny:

Jenny can see her side of the dance they have around sex. She has been the one with the lower desire for sex all along. She shows up, occasionally, and has sex out of obligation. Caught in the typical desire discrepancy trap of the person with more desire, Rich derives validation—a sense of security and desirability—when they have sex, but he gets moody and withdrawn when they don't. She is turned off by his emotional state. She has never spoken up about this before. And while she didn't realize it until now, she is also turned off by the meaning sex has at this point—making him feel better. She is also coming to realize that she has come to take advantage of the control over sex that she has as the person with lower desire, and she gets a sense of power out of rejecting sex. It is this wielding of control that gives her the only feeling of power she has in the relationship. Jenny recognizes that she is punishing Rich for a break up early in their relationship.

Jenny came from a family in which her dad was an alcoholic. Her home was chaotic and unpredictable. Her dad wasn't an angry or violent drunk, but her mom would enable her dad's drinking. The whole household revolved around taking care of dad when he was drunk; from not mentioning the alcohol to covering him up with a blanket when he passed out on the couch. Jenny internalized the message that mom couldn't handle anything else. She learned to keep quiet and fly under the radar. The last thing she would consider was speaking up about something she wanted.

Jenny can tell that, in a way, she has become her mother. Like so many other children of alcoholics, she's become vigilant, codependent, and detached from her own desires. She's been enabling Rich's strategy of finding validation through sex. Jenny has given up her own wants (sexual and otherwise), and she's adopted a service role in the relationship. She hasn't found her own voice, but she has found a way to exert power in a passive-aggressive way—by withholding sex. She also recognizes that she's been hiding behind the kids. The children provide plenty of excuses for her exhaustion and stress. While the kids have legitimate needs, she has put those up as a wall to justify not prioritizing her marriage and her intimate life.

Jenny needs to learn to access her own desires, in sex and out, and begin to take up space in the relationship. She also has to acknowledge the anger she feels, not just at her parents, but at Rich. That early breakup was unexpected and painful, and she's harbored both fear and anger ever since. She'll have to make a conscious choice to stop holding that against him and work on their sex life. She recognizes that she has associated doing what somebody else wants with giving up her power—a zero sum game. Jenny needs to change that mindset and learn to choose to have sex, instead of doing it because she must.

Rich:

Rich grew up in a home where his parents were disconnected. They didn't communicate well, although they didn't fight. They were more the silent couple, going about life on autopilot. He never saw his parents share physical affection. There seemed to be no passion. However, they were devoted to raising the children. It was a shock to him when they divorced after he graduated from high school. Looking back on it now, it seems silly to him that it shocked him. He can see how he learned as a kid to put on blinders to what was going on right in front of him. He now knows he's developed a fear that relationships will fall apart. He has a constant feeling like the rug is about to be pulled out from under him.

Rich has a history of anxiety. It is not troubling enough to require medication, but he has a long history of worry and ruminating thoughts. As a result, he tends to catastrophize, so when things don't go well between Jenny and him, he gets panicky and certain their relationship can't get better. He needs to regulate his own emotions and anxiety.

Going over his relationship history, he realizes that his other girlfriends had all either cheated on him or been the ones to break up. He can see how this has affected his self-esteem and caused him to doubt himself. He recognizes that he has an intense need for validation and reassurance that gets activated every time Jenny isn't interested in sex. Rich needs to learn to separate his sense of worth from her sexual desire. He also needs to embrace her growing ability to say no and not see that as personal rejection.

Lastly, Rich admits that he has resentment towards the kids. Jenny has used them as a shield for so long that he has displaced his anger with her onto them. He has purposely been less involved in the household, especially when it comes to kid duties, because he's angry. He needs to separate the feelings he has about Jenny and his marriage from how he operates with the children. Only then can he step into a full parenting role and develop healthy, strong relationships with both of his kids.

Tom and Grant

Tom and Grant are in their 30s and in a newer relationship. They want penetrative sex, partly thinking it's the "right" kind, but neither knows how to talk about it. Grant views their sexual problems as a sign that they shouldn't be together, and Tom has developed ED from the pressure of the situation.

Tom:

Tom's parents ran a strict household, and there was a lot of daily conflict. Dad was the boss, and Mom generally backed him up with the kids, although she fought him on plenty of other things. By the time he was a teenager, Tom was spending as much time away from home, with friends and at activities, as he could. The anger and fighting were very stressful to him. As a result, he is highly conflict-avoidant now. He also tends to be the "pursuer" in relationship; he wants to stay close, repair misunderstandings, and is uncomfortable with any level of upset in his partner. He needs to increase his tolerance for negative emotions and change his reaction to conflict so that he can have healthy disagreement and resolution.

Tom grew up in an area of the country where it was not safe to be gay. He witnessed and experienced some horrific abuse by other high school boys when he was a teenager, and those events still haunt him. His family was religious and conservative, and it was clearly not okay with them to be gay, either. Once his parents figured out he was gay (by finding gay porn on his computer and confronting him), they sent him into conversion therapy for a year. It was an awful and traumatizing experience. Eventually, when he didn't "repent" or "change his mind," his family cut him off. He hasn't spoken to them for almost 15 years, except for very brief communication with his sister.

These experiences have left him with a lingering sense of shame and confusion about sex and his own sexuality. His parents never talked about sex, and certainly not about how people of the same gender might share sex. The sex education he had, like so much of it across the country, only mentioned heterosexual sex. He learned early on not to talk about sex or to ask questions. It wasn't until after he left for college in a different part of the country that he began to have sex with other people and tried to figure some of this out for himself.

As described earlier, Tom has had some penetrative sex but only with partners who at least seemed to know what they were doing. He never spoke up in those situations about what felt good or what he wanted. He took the approach of both hoping they'd figure it out and just not seeing people again if it didn't work well.

He has no experience having hard conversations or being direct about his concerns. He needs to release the shame of his upbringing and start to explore what he really wants in sex. He needs to learn to talk about sex with Grant.

Tom freezes with anxiety when Grant gets upset. He's got to learn to settle himself down and not feed into the negative energy. He feels dread at the thought of sex, and he's starting to avoid it. He must tell Grant what his concerns are and ask to work it out together.

Tom also needs to shift his expectations to realize that sex, at least good sex, must be learned. He and Grant need to talk about what might work and know that it's okay to spend time and experimentation to have the sex they want. He also needs to expand his sense of what sex is, letting go of the heteronormative idea that penetration is the standard by which sex is judged. It's one thing to want anal sex, but it isn't okay to feel like anything else you enjoy isn't enough.

Grant:

Grant also grew up in a family where emotions ran hot. His mother was manipulative and controlling. Grant has moved 3000 miles away to escape her influence. His dad was a drinker and was frequently out all night. He suspects his father had many affairs but doesn't know for sure. The worse his father's behavior became, the more his mother locked onto Grant and tried to make him into a dutiful son and confidante. Grant can see that his silly, joking way of dealing with sex mirrors the way he approached his intense family—using humor as avoidance.

While both Tom and Grant come from high conflict families, they have adopted different strategies regarding conflict. While Tom can't leave bad feelings unresolved, Grant can see that he withdraws from conflict and has become the "distancer" in relationship. Closeness feels threatening to him. When he and Tom have disagreements, he tends to stay calm for a while but then explode with anger. He would rather avoid issues entirely than risk getting into heated arguments or long, painful, and draining discussions. He recognizes that he must deal directly with issues and moderate his emotions instead of copying the intense reactivity modeled in his family. Grant has to find a way to approach and interact with Tom when they struggle, instead of following his instinct to withdraw.

Grant's family was also conservative and not supportive of his sexual orientation, although they've accepted it at this point and maintain a relationship with him. It was an unspoken thing when he was growing up, so Grant internalized a sense of shame about being gay. He's had several past sexual partners, but this is his first real long-term relationship. He has taken pride as a lover in the past; he's gotten a lot of positive affirmation. He has a belief that you shouldn't have to talk about sex if you're with the right person. He has wanted to have penetrative sex before, but he never brought it up or tried with anyone else. He is nervous about it, and his nervousness manifests in high reactivity when it doesn't go well. He can see how his emotional outbursts aren't helping the situation and are a major contributor to Tom's erection issues. He needs to get a handle on his emotions and stay settled. Grant also needs to drop the expectation that he doesn't need to communicate about sex.

SECTION 3:

THE ACTION PLAN

CHAPTER 10

Put Insight into Action

A large part the book up to now deals with working on insight—understanding what is happening in your mind, your relationships, and your sex life. You've had a chance to challenge your thinking about what sex is and what it can be. You learned specific attitudes and actions that create a vibrant, healthy relationship and sex life. You've examined your past to uncover your patterns of belief and behavior. You've seen the importance of confronting yourself and cleaning up your own side of the court, and you have put together concrete ideas about what you need to change to improve your sexual relationship. Hopefully, you are starting to have a vision of sex as a fun, intimate possibility in your lives. These are a lot of changes that have happened in your mind.

But insight doesn't equal change. Change comes from deciding to behave differently. Ultimately, you need to change how you act and what you do. Change is experiential. You need to practice new ways of being and behaving. To help you do this, I am first going to describe the primary tool I use for change, the Giver/Receiver Exercise, and then provide you, in the next chapter, my tried and tested 9-phase plan for taking the stress out of sex. It is time for more work—the healthy work to help you change insight into action, and action into new behaviors.

The Giver/Receiver exercise will be your tool.

This exercise is a great place for the experiential work you need to do to change your sex life. Here, you can practice everything we've talked about so far. Even though it is contrived and may feel awkward, an exercise gives you a framework for change. It is time limited. It is focused on specific tasks. The rules are (relatively) clear. Each person has a job (again)! This exercise gives you a chance to experiment and learn. It is an experience meant to evoke responses that give you information about where you struggle. That is the point—you get to sit with your experience, notice what comes up for you, and learn more about what's in your own way. Then you can use it to change how you're thinking and what you're doing. It becomes the laboratory where you change the dynamics.

DIRECTIONS

For 10 minutes each, one of you will be the Receiver and one the Giver. The Receiver is in charge for that 10-minute stretch. Set an alarm so you don't have to be looking at a clock. The Receiver asks for and directs the Giver to provide whatever type of physical touch will feel best to the Receiver in the moment. The Receiver should talk through most of their turn, directing and giving feedback so the Giver can provide as "perfect" a touch as possible. The Receiver retains "ownership" of their experience, not passing responsibility to the Giver to know what to do or to create the experience.

Concentrate on letting go of all expectations. The touch can be sexual or non-sexual. There is absolutely no expectation that either of you become aroused, and there is certainly no goal of orgasm. It is not necessary to match each other's choices during your turns as the Receiver; you can want and request vastly different forms of touch. The exercise is a study in moment-by-moment pleasure, with no attachment to an outcome.

The Receiver's Jobs:

1. Access desire.

Whether you know what you want or whether it's
hard to come up with anything, part of your work
as the Receiver is to find pleasure in touch.

2. Ask for what you want.

Ask for exactly what you want and give instruction and feedback.
This requires being explicit and specific—enough so the Giver
knows exactly what you want them to do. The intention is to ask
for what would be best for you, without censoring yourself at all.
Let go of trying to please your partner or keeping them in their
comfort zone. This is a chance for it to be only about you. (The
Giver has their own job of saying no, if necessary, so the Receiver is freed from taking care of the other person. If the Giver
says no to your request, you should just pick something else.)

3. Allow yourself to receive.

Be present with the touch. Relax and enjoy. Take as much
delight or pleasure as you can in receiving touch.

4. Pay attention to your experience.

Notice what it is like for you in your turn as the Receiver.
Did you ask for the touch you really wanted? Did you censor
yourself? Could you articulate what you wanted? Was it difficult to
receive? Were there things you noticed in your partner that had an
impact on you?

The Giver's Jobs:

1. Say no if you NEED to say no.

You need to say no if the request will be painful or physically uncomfortable in a way you don't like. You also need to say no if providing the Receiver's requested touch will be upsetting or traumatic to you. If you do need to say no, the Receiver should just pick something else. Only you can discern whether you *need* to say no or just *want* to.

2. If you just WANT to say no, then choose to do it anyway.

If your first reaction is to want to say no, thinking things like, "I'm not sure I like this," "I am not really in the mood for this," "this makes me anxious," or "I'm not sure how I feel about this; we haven't done it before," then I ask you to choose to do it anyway. It may get worse, at which point you can say no, but getting out of your comfort zone is where the real work is. In this case, you will learn more about where your discomfort comes from and, over time, whether you can shift that response at all.

3. If it's neutral or easy to do, see if you can get in an open-hearted space of wanting to give.

It is not necessarily easy to feel generous with your partner. But this is a chance to practice inhabiting a space of generosity, working to want to provide the "perfect" touch your partner is requesting.

4. Pay attention to your experience.

Notice what it's like for you in the role of Giver. Did you need to say no? What thoughts and feelings arose as you were in the exercise? What light does that shed on where your challenges are? Were you able to feel openness and generosity? Did you read anything in your partner that had an impact on you?

When the alarm goes off, stop no matter what you are doing. Remember that there was no goal with the 10-minute turn, so you don't need to finish anything. Switch roles and do the other 10 minutes. Again, when the alarm goes off, stop there. That is the entire exercise, and you can stop wherever you are. You have the option of doing it again, spending more intimate time together, or having sex, but that should be a separate decision, not considered or made until the 20 minutes is over.

Here are some important notes for the Giver/Receiver exercise.

You can't do this wrong. This exercise is first meant to get information: what are your obstacles? What thoughts or feelings come up and shed light on where you are starting? What challenges can you focus on next time? You don't need to argue over the instructions or feel like you're failing. No matter what happens, you get information.

Don't be discouraged if things seem to go badly. I think of this exercise, in its early use, as getting the monsters to come out from under the bed. Instead of being a way around your sexual issues, this exercise will take you straight *through* them. If it's hard, that means the exercise is working. The struggles you have are not a coincidence; they relate directly to the issues in your sex life. Each time you do the exercise, you have the opportunity to grow and change. That said, do be mindful of pacing. While you want to stretch yourself, you do not want to break. It's okay if the exercise is hard, but it shouldn't feel traumatic or disastrous.

It takes intention to do this on a regular basis. If you say, "We should do the exercise," it is unlikely to happen. There is no "should" used in taking action, and don't wait for "we." I encourage each of you to take ownership of it, suggesting it in a concrete way. I suggest language such as "I want to do the exercise" or "this is important to me." Suggest it in a moment when you can do it or be concrete and suggest a specific time in the next day or so.

You do not have to be feeling great to do the exercise. While I recommend not leaving it until last thing before bed (when so many people are likely to be exhausted), you can do this exercise in any mood and with any amount of energy. Part of what you get out of the exercise is a chance to practice shifting gears, showing up, and becoming present and open. If you are feeling down about your partner, use this opportunity to find the warmth you have toward them that's under the surface. If you are tired, you can participate with less energy, but still work to bring yourself to the activity. If you are distracted or stressed, you can use the time to practice letting go of those thoughts and try to engage with your partner.

The more you do this, the more you will get out of it. This exercise has subtlety to it. There are layers of information you can uncover because each time you try the exercise, it is slightly different. As you learn more about your individual challenges, each repetition of the exercise gives you a chance to practice moving further along. And because you are doing this with a partner, their experience and growth affects you, too. Take your time with this. Allow your experiences to unfold slowly.

Keep in mind that each of you is responsible for your own side of the court. Don't focus on your partner's issues; avoid the temptation to help them manage their growth. Focus on your own issues, working to make progress each time you repeat the exercise. Know what you're trying to improve each time you do it.

The exercise will mirror some of the desire politics of your relationship. You will probably encounter the same pattern around initiation of the exercise that you have with sex. Figure out who is the partner with the higher desire for the exercise and who has the lower. Think about how that is likely to impact you bringing it up or doing it. Anticipate the challenges that come from the pattern with your partner, and plan ahead to navigate those differences. Resolve to approach this differently than you've approached sex so far.

Use the exercise for growth.

The utility of this exercise is not just in the doing, but also in the reflection on what happened for you and the debriefing with your partner. Whatever happens, pay attention. The key to your own growth is in your reactions to the exercise. You will likely notice the challenges that surface directly relate to issues you have in your sex life. This is a chance to begin making things different.

When I'm working with clients in therapy, we debrief the exercise together and strategize about how to use the information that comes from it. To set you up for success to do this on your own, I'm going to lay out a way to use the exercise in a progressive way, addressing some of the main tenets of a successful sex life along the way. The next chapter will take you through these ideas and will show you how the exercise can help you master each one.

CHAPTER 11

The 9 Phases of Taking the Stress Out of Sex

There are some key skills and attitudes that are fundamental to a healthy and thriving sex life. The Giver/Receiver exercise can be used to practice and integrate all of them. In my therapy practice, my clients are working to develop all these skills at once, but here you can move through them as separate phases. Focus on one at a time and learn how the exercise can help you master each one. The directions for the exercise never change, but you use it to emphasize the development of different competencies in order to grow.

Give yourself plenty of time with each phase. There is no quick fix here. You might decide to spend a certain number of weeks with each area of focus. Or you could decide to do the exercise a certain number of times before you move on to the next step. There is not a test to know when to progress to the next phase. Use your judgment about how to proceed to make the most impact on your unique challenge. All these concepts are at play at the same time, so it's a matter of intentionally focusing on one thing at a time to help you master and integrate each skill.

As you go along, add the newest area of focus on top of the others, so that by the end, you're working to integrate all the different aspects of a great sex life at the same time. Realize that while I have laid this out in phases building on each other, you may find that you'll want to work in a different order, depending on what challenges come up for you and your partner. You and your partner can focus on different aspects, too, since your work is different. I've put this together in an order I have found to be most useful with my clients over the years, but please know it is merely a suggestion. Work with this information in the way that seems most helpful and relevant to you and your situation.

Phase 1—Prioritizing Intimacy

People can put sex far down on the priority list. As you have kids, get busy with careers, or deal with other challenges life throws you, you often decide that sex can wait. You may feel like your partner can wait, too, especially compared to the young kids who need so much of your attention or the job demands that must be addressed. A lot of people would prefer to just get some sleep! Sex becomes something you do only when you have extra time and energy.

Early on in a relationship, sex is often automatically a top priority. It doesn't need any forethought, planning, or convincing to make it happen. As you are getting to know your partner, falling in love, and in that discovery phase, you may have easy access to your desire for sex. It takes no work or intention. It happens with a decent frequency, and neither person has to think too much about it. As the newness wears off, you get more comfortable. Life tends to get in the way, and sex drops down the list unless you put intention into having it more often.

If sex doesn't come easily in the beginning, you may think, "It will get better with time, I just need to deal with some other things first." Perhaps you believe you need to let your attraction grow if you started more as friends. Or you just need to learn about each other. Whatever the underlying issue, you think that somehow it will work itself out. However, if time keeps passing without any improvement in your sex life, you may question whether you're sexually compatible or if you should even be together. Regardless of how the sexual relationship started, without effort to make your sex life work, it can wither over time.

Nothing will change until you do something different. If you and your partner have been avoiding your sex life, then the other parts of life have taken over all your available time. If you intend to make things better, you're going to have to prioritize intimacy.

One of the most important things you can do is be intentional about intimate time with your partner.

I recommend you create an "anchor" time in which you spend anywhere from 5 to 30 minutes together every day. This can become a ritual and something to look forward to. It gives you a chance to talk and connect or just relax together and share space. It could be a time when you incorporate physical or sexual touch, too. Whether it's over a cup of coffee in the morning, a glass of wine or a cup of tea in the evening, or walking the dog together every night, make sure you are getting some amount of uninterrupted couple time each day. If you aren't in the same location, then make that happen by phone or video.

Date nights and trips are also wonderful opportunities to invest in your relationship. It is great to have longer couple time to go out and have fun. (Laughter does wonders!) Plan some dates, get a sitter for the kids, and make sure you're out doing new and interesting things together if you can. Find a frequency that works for your life and your budget, but there are ways to do it cheaply. Whatever effort and money you spend to make this happen, it's much cheaper than divorce and easier than a break up. Your investment in your relationship will pay off.

It's also important to prioritize time and energy to be physically intimate together. One of the first obstacles you will encounter is that you must make this happen. Since you are struggling in your sex life, you (or your partner) may well have developed some avoidance when it comes to being physically involved. You may resist the idea of scheduling sex, but if you've been avoiding your sex life, you're going to have to change that on purpose. And it's not sex you're scheduling. You're scheduling a "trip to the playground," like I talked about in Chapter 4. No expectations and no pressure—just an outing with your partner where you can have fun. You schedule the opportunity; the rest happens as it will. You can certainly still have spontaneous encounters—that's great—but those can be in addition to what you've planned.

Getting around to sex can feel like the way people often treat exercise. When you're together for a long time, you often go through stages where it feels like work to have sex. And since you and your partner have been in a cycle of avoiding sex, it's definitely work to tackle the things that have made you avoid it in the first place. So on top of the mental and emotional work of dealing with your issues and expectations, you've got to summon the energy to climb the stairs, take off your clothes, *and* somehow get your mind involved! If you are in a stage like that now, then go ahead treat it like exercise.

Commit to it. Make yourself show up in the right state of undress. Just get going. Don't worry about the outcome or expectations. If you only make one lap around the track, at least you tried. In these stages, it's about making a habit and a commitment to show up, whether intrinsically driven or not. Just like exercise, the early days of trying to change your sex life may involve some resistance. That's when it's important to keep showing up so you get stronger. Just like exercise, once you start making progress, good sex will energize you and make it that much easier to get engaged the next time. Eventually, it's not going to feel like work anymore. Desire can ebb and flow, so the important thing is to adapt to those fluctuations and maintain some momentum in your intimate life.

I encourage you to decide now if you are invested in this process. Do you think it is worth the effort? Are you committed to making change? If the answers are yes, then start saying things like, "I want to do this. Can we spend the time together tonight at 8 p.m.?" Be concrete and take the initiative to suggest it (repeatedly if necessary). If both of you do this, the odds of success go way up.

Another common pitfall in prioritizing intimacy is leaving it until the end of the night or putting it after everything else on your to-do list. If you haven't managed to create time together with your partner, sit down and strategize together about where this time is going to come from. If it hasn't been a regular part of your life, something else is going to have to give. Try some different times of day. Schedule this in a time slot before you are exhausted.

Using the Receiver Exercise—Prioritizing Intimacy

Avoidance can be deep-rooted, and it's going to take effort to make something happen when you've spent so much time avoiding your intimate life. When starting to work with the Giver/Receiver Exercise, you will likely run into the same issues of time and initiation that plague your sex life. You can use this exercise to begin creating space for intimacy in your life. As you figure out how you're going to fit the exercise into your life, you're shifting to make intimacy a priority. You can begin by doing the exercise in that "anchor" time of day you've already created. The bonus is that the exercise becomes somewhat of a placeholder for you: time that will be available for other forms of intimacy and connection once your sex life has improved and you no longer need the exercise. (However, you may want to continue doing it occasionally just as a refresher.)

PITFALL: NOT DOING THE EXERCISE

You may completely forget about the plan to do the exercise. Or you think about it but avoid bringing it up. Perhaps you notice that your partner doesn't seem interested or comfortable, so you decide not to push it. You think they should be the one to drive this, so you sit back and wait for them to step up. You take the same approach to the exercise as you do to sex, falling into the usual pattern of not tackling it head on.

BREAKTHROUGH: HOLDING YOURSELF
ACCOUNTABLE AND GETTING IT DONE

You commit to change and determine to speak up about the exercise no matter what. You bring it up in concrete ways and with a clear request that you'd like to do it. You ask about it even if you read your partner as not wanting to do it; you allow them to make the choice about doing it with you or not. You also hold them accountable if they keep putting it off, reminding them of your mutual commitment to change.

Phase 2—Communicating About Sex

Good communication is a key component of a satisfying sex life. For many people, talking about sex is difficult and uncomfortable. If you are struggling with your sex life, you often either avoid the topic or argue in circles until a fight flares up. You may have been raised in a household where sex wasn't discussed. Because you didn't get any modeling for how to talk about sex, you internalized the message that it's not an appropriate topic of conversation. Your sex education, if you had any, probably didn't include information on talking about pleasure, connection, variety, and exploration with a partner—the topics that are critically important to tending to your sex life. If you were lucky enough to be raised in a sexually open and healthy environment, or you have some comfort with talking about sex regardless of your taboo upbringing, your partner may not have that same willingness to talk about things.

Maybe you didn't need to talk about sex much early in your relationship. After all, there's a lot you can do and enjoy without needing to talk about it. You can signal your wishes with body language, movement, and vocalization. You can get by on this tactic for quite a while, depending on how things are going and how well you are matched to your partner. But over time, and as things change (or one of you is interested in changing what you're doing), it becomes more important to be able to address sex directly.

If you are in a place where problems and negative feelings are already a factor, talking about sex is even more important. Unfortunately, it is also even more difficult. If neither of you has the skills or willingness to talk about difficult topics like sex, you will probably end up avoiding it.

Communicating about sex has more than one layer to it. You need the ability to talk about your sex life as a whole: its role in your life, your overall satisfaction, your expectations, your disappointments, and your contribution to the problems you're experiencing. That's what you addressed in Section 2 of this book. But you also will need, at some point, to be able to talk specifically about the act of sex itself: what you like, what you want, how things feel, and where your boundaries are. These conversations need to be specific and explicit. They don't have to be lengthy, but you need to be able to talk to your partner clearly enough that they understand.

Ask for things. Tell your partner what you'd like. Provide feedback, encouragement, and instruction. Invite the same from your partner. The more you can create a dialogue about what is working, what you want, and how to best move through sex together, the more you will be able to optimize your physical experience and create a sense of partnership and connection with your lover. You don't need to talk your way through every sexual encounter, but getting used to communicating about and during sex means you can use words when you need them.

One technique I suggest is reading a good, approachable sex book aloud to each other (you could read from the titles I share at the end of the book). This way, you start out reading about sex in the abstract. You're not talking about yourself yet, so it can feel less threatening. Doing this helps you get used to the language of sex, desensitizing you in the process. Plus, you may learn a few things and get some ideas about what you want in sex.

Using the Receiver Exercise— Communicating about sex

You can use the Giver/Receiver Exercise to practice talking about how you like to be touched. Because you are asked to direct your partner, almost continuously, you can learn to overcome your reluctance to ask for things and to be specific in your requests. While you will probably not talk that much during "regular" sex, having the ability to speak up and be specific when necessary is a good tool to have in your toolbox.

PITFALL: NOT BEING ABLE TO ASK FOR WHAT YOU WANT

You know what you want, but you feel ashamed, self-conscious, or just embarrassed to be that specific. You've never been comfortable talking about sex. You've never learned to give feedback. You don't know what to call your body parts, and it feels awkward to be specific, directive, or "bossy." You've always believed your partner should be able to read you. Or maybe they should know what you want. Or you're worried that your partner is so uncomfortable with sexual talk that you clam up. So you tone down or change what you want. Or give vague instructions. Or lapse into silence and hand the control over to the Giver.

BREAKTHROUGH: GETTING COMFORTABLE TALKING ABOUT SEX

You get a lot of practice giving feedback and putting what you want into words. You learn the level of specificity you need to get the desired result. You learn how you want to refer to various parts of your body. You can speak up easily when you want something different because you've gotten good at talking during a physical encounter.

Phase 3—Accessing Desire

Good sex involves wanting. Desire is fundamental to an enjoyable encounter. But one or both of you may not have wanted intimacy in a long time. Desire may be something for which you need to go searching.

While desire may have come naturally early on in your relationship, you tend to have to cultivate it, at least sometimes, in a long-term relationship. Most couples who have been together a while have a basic way they have sex. (You've already talked about yours in the previous section of this book.) There may be some variation, but you likely have settled in to an effective way of meeting your goals—whether that is an orgasm for one or both, just getting it done quickly, or something else. You may have gotten (and given) feedback along the way that some sexual activities are off the table, resulting in a lowest common denominator aspect to your sexual repertoire. It's easy to get into a rut or a routine when it comes to sex. That can lead to both people not even thinking about what else they'd like. And it can result in a lukewarm attitude toward sex, with no sense of urgency.

This kind of complacency will cause even more of a problem if one or both of you experience the reactive type of desire I described in Chapter 3. Reactive sexual desire requires a willingness to start, to see what will happen, and to hold the idea that you want intimate connection even if you are not feeling interested in the moment. You need to create the opportunities for sexual desire to arise. If you and your partner get lazy or complacent, or if you start saying no because you aren't in the mood at that moment, your sex life can stagnate. You start missing the opportunities to connect with your partner sexually. If you start saying no because you're trapped in a negative cycle, or out of fear about how your lack of response will play out between the two of you, sex gets especially difficult. Do you say no to sex because you don't feel like having sex at that moment and can't really imagine getting in the mood?

In fact, many of you start avoiding any physical affection at all because you want to avoid being put on the spot and turning your partner down again. You don't want to leave your partner hanging or come off as a "tease." Moments of sexual initiation can become loaded with negative feelings and are often the source of distance or fighting between you and your partner. This is a common way people start avoiding sex in the first place.

You may have struggled to ever want *anything*. Many people struggle with desire in general. You grow up in an environment that teaches you whether your desires are valued, whether there is room for your wishes, whether you can expect to have your wants fulfilled, and whether your voice can be heard and welcomed. You may have learned not to want because it was equated with neediness. Depending on your background, you may have turned off *wanting* a very long time ago. You may have convinced yourself that you can't expect anything, maybe from anyone. You may have learned to be completely independent and self-sufficient a long time ago. It's not that those traits are bad, but if it means you can't access desire, it creates a problem for your intimate life.

You may also struggle with wanting sex because of relationship issues between you and your partner, be they sexual or otherwise. You'll have to tackle those issues—bring them up and resolve them—to be able to want to have sex again. Cultivating and welcoming desire is a critical part of satisfying sex.

I suggest you and your partner practice stating your desires on a regular basis, in small ways, about everyday things. From figuring out what to do for dinner to how you want to spend a weekend afternoon, you have lots of opportunity to find and express what you want. I recommend you each state what you want first, before deciding what you will do. Use the words "I want" or "I would like" so you demonstrate ownership of your own desires. Once each of you has said what you want, then you can decide together what to do.

If you find it especially difficult to access and communicate your own desires, I recommend using poker chips as a tool. Put 10 chips in your pocket; each represents one statement of desire. Every time you come across them in your pocket, you'll be reminded that you need to find an opportunity to express what you want. If you and your partner are both doing this, you can give each other chips as you make statements of desire. This makes it obvious that you are making a conscious effort to express your wish. If you're doing it alone, just move a chip out of your pocket with each desire that you express. Remember that just because you say you want something, it doesn't mean you're going to get it. This is also a way to practice tolerating a no.

I also recommend that you stop having a black and white, yes or no response to sex and enter the grey area of *maybe*. You can let your partner know that you weren't really thinking about sex, but that you're willing to give it a try and see what happens. Perhaps your motor will turn over, perhaps not. It starts with a willingness to engage in any sort of sexual encounter—kissing, touching, whatever. It is important for you both to let go of attachment to any particular outcome, to learn to enjoy the moment for what it offers. Go slowly, relax, and experiment with what it takes to connect with your partner and feel good about what you're doing. You may find that you or your partner need more information or more practice in what to do and how to do it in a way that will be pleasing. Willingness to enter a sexual space together and to explore, in this context, is not an agreement to end up doing any specific thing, like intercourse. And because it isn't, there can be room to say maybe, which is a yes to getting started.

Using the Receiver Exercise—Accessing desire

You can use the Giver/Receiver Exercise to work on these issues. Your 10-minute turn as the Receiver is an invitation to take the time to figure out what you might like. If you don't know, start with anything and go from there. Pick a random place on your body and some sort of touch and see what you might want next. As you proceed, notice how it feels and be receptive to any ideas you have about what might feel better. You can use the exercise to explore touch and figure out what you want. You don't have to know ahead of time.

If you do have ideas, practice asking for them—with enough specificity and explicitness that you get what you really want. Notice where you hold back and try to overcome that. Your turn is also a place to become progressively more comfortable receiving. Over time, you can access more desire for touch and increase your comfort with wanting.

PITFALL 1: NOT KNOWING WHAT YOU WANT

You may not know what you want. Maybe you've never known what you want. You may feel like sex has never been about you or you've never had the chance to explore your own body. If you struggle with lack of sexual desire, you may have a hard time finding any pleasure in your body or touch at all. If you've experienced sexual trauma in the past, this can block your desire to be touched or to be sexual. You may be facing a blank slate when it comes to finding touch you'd enjoy.

You may not know what you want because things have changed. As you get older, your body and responses change, so sometimes it feels like you're in a body you don't know. If you've had surgery, illness, or disability, your body may not be like the one you'd gotten used to. It can feel like your body has betrayed you. Or you might be happy with your new body but not yet know how you want to use it.

BREAKTHROUGH 1: LEARNING WHAT YOU WANT

You learn more about what feels good. You explore new things that you never considered. You explore your entire body (not just focusing on genitals). You also explore your genitals in a new way, not just doing the same things as before. You discover new kinds of touch, and you learn things you never knew you liked. Your body surprises you.

PITFALL 2: STRUGGLING TO WANT

It's uncomfortable to be in the position of Receiver. You're more comfortable thinking about pleasing someone else and focusing on their desires. You anticipate being disappointed, so you struggle to ask for what you want. You try to avoid the heartbreak you expect, thinking your partner won't be willing to do what you ask. You feel exposed if you reveal your desires, and you worry that what you want will let your partner down. You believe (or pretend) that there's nothing you'd like in the exercise. You participate in your partner's turn as Receiver but don't take yours.

BREAKTHROUGH 2: ALLOWING YOURSELF TO WANT

You accept that there are ways you like to be touched, and you are open to learning more about them. You allow yourself to look forward to your turn as the Receiver. You are willing to reveal your preferences. You face the possibility of disappointment more easily, still letting your desires exist and maintaining hope that your wants can be met. You take your turn as the Receiver. You stop worrying about whether your wants meet your partner's expectations; you're able to feel good about them because they're yours. You start to feel empowered in your desires.

Phase 4—Enjoying the Journey

Being attached to the outcome is a common problem in sex. A lot of people assume that the goal of sex is orgasm. It's nice to be able to have an orgasm if you want one but focusing on that as the end goal has its problems.

First, not everyone can have an orgasm, at least not every time. If that's your goal for either yourself or your partner, you are set up to fail, at least some of the time. Your body changes, and your responsiveness fluctuates, so there's no way you're going to bat 1000. And focusing on orgasm often makes it harder to reach one, especially if that's combined with any worry or self-consciousness about your performance.

Shooting for a goal like that also minimizes the rest of the experience. Anything but that seems "less than." The rest of the encounter is just used to reach the orgasm, without value by itself. You may not be paying attention to the rest of the experience; you don't savor or relish all the sensations. You can be so focused on moving forward that you are in the future moment, not the present one. Don't rush your way through the foreplay to get to the main event. Most of you have an efficient way of having sex; often that's exactly because you're doing what moves you toward orgasm the most quickly. If that's the goal, and especially if you are pressed for time or energy, you tend to want to do only what's needed to get there and nothing more.

Achieving the goal of orgasm may feel like enough of a payoff to keep you interested in sex, at least for a while. But you or your partner may get bored, even though you reach orgasm. It may not seem much more fulfilling than masturbating, and masturbating may be less trouble. And if you start to struggle to be interested, to get aroused, or to reach orgasm, you will likely start to feel bad about sex.

As I described earlier, my take on a healthy view of sex is that it is about pleasure and connection, in varying proportions. Focus on orgasm often makes it difficult to be present in the moment, and it can create pressure and anxiety for one or both partners if sex isn't a straight line from initiation to arousal to orgasm. Sex is dramatically enhanced when you stop being destination-oriented and start enjoying each step along the journey. It is great fun to play in the space before orgasm: allowing arousal to build, subside, and build again. New possibilities open when you are not driving directly to climax. And if you or your partner struggle with arousal or orgasm, taking the focus off the outcome and learning to enjoy touch and connection allows you to enjoy what you're doing (and may very well make it easier to reach orgasm later if you want to).

This attitude will serve you well if you ever encounter changes in your life that affect your (or your partner's) sexual functioning. Whether you have a permanent change at some point or are just faced with a night where you're too tired to be as responsive as usual, you have more options for pleasure and connection if you enjoy what is without worrying about what may follow.

If you have never had an orgasm or regularly struggle to reach one, it's worth doing what you can to make that an option, but that still doesn't mean it should be the focus of your sexual interactions or the marker of success. You may want to work on discovering your way to climax through masturbation or through practice sessions with your partner where that is the focus—but that can be separate from sex where you try not to have a goal. Pull back on the expectations, assume it will not happen right away, and take your time. Then make sure to also have sex where that pressure is off the table.

One reason you may struggle to just enjoy the journey is the concern about what will happen if you want to stop part way through. The fear of disappointing or frustrating your partner can prevent you from even starting to be sexual. To help you address this concern and allow you to relax and enjoy, I encourage you to develop "other endings" that work for both of you in case one of you is really aroused and the other isn't. At each moment during a sexual encounter, including one that started with a maybe, each of you has the choice to continue or not. You choose whether to turn up the heat or to dial it back. The important part is sharing a sexual moment; it is less important what you do together. At some point, you may find yourself aroused and interested in sex. Great! If not, you can collaborate on other endings that can feel satisfying to you both. Once you both realize that there is more than one outcome that feels like a success, the easier it's going to be to dive in and see what happens. Creating more opportunity to get aroused will likely lead to more sex, but there will still be times where your motor doesn't turn over. You need to have a variety of ways to wrap up these encounters and feel good about them.

What can you do if sex, however you have it, does not end up as an option? There are more solutions to that than you can imagine. Some of them may require practice, patience, or personal growth. If you aren't aroused, but your partner is interested in an orgasm, there are a lot of ways to solve that. You can be as actively involved in their orgasm as you want to be.

- You can bring them to orgasm (through oral sex, manual stimulation, use of a vibrator or any other means).

- They can masturbate, putting in all the effort themselves, while you are present with them.

- You can share the "work" of whatever stimulation it would take for your partner to climax. For instance, you can nibble their ear or nipple while they use their hands on their own genitals. You can both be stroking their genitals together. You can take turns doing the stroking that they find pleasurable. There are innumerable ways to work together on their pleasure.

- You can let arousal naturally fade and not pursue an orgasm. There are tantric practices that feature this kind of energy build-up over days; many people find it enjoyable and invigorating.

Just because you both don't want to end an encounter with sex (or with two orgasms) doesn't mean you need to *avoid* sexual interaction. It is helpful to have a variety of ways to conclude a sexual encounter that work for both of you—even if this takes working through inhibitions. Practicing flexibility by having any number of ways to share sexual interaction reduces a lot of pressure and creates the opportunity for your sexual relationship to thrive.

Using the Receiver Exercise— Enjoying the journey

You can use the Giver/Receiver Exercise to practice letting go of expectation and outcome. Because the exercise is time limited, and because you are asked to immerse yourself in the moment and let go of any goal of arousal or orgasm for you and your partner, you have the opportunity to take a new kind of journey together. This becomes a model for how you can approach sex: where you have the option to reach orgasm but don't have to worry about it ahead of time, where you can linger in the spaces before climax and explore the breadth of sexual experience, where you can still connect with your partner in pleasure even if orgasm, or even arousal, is off the table for one or both of you. It's also a place to practice those other endings, since sometimes one of you may end up aroused and interested in continued pleasure or orgasm once the exercise is over. I invite you to see what it's like to let go of the outcome and just enjoy yourselves!

PITFALL: BEING ATTACHED TO A GOAL

You can't get over the idea that you should get aroused. Or that you want an orgasm (or to give one). Or that you really want to have sex after the exercise is over. It's hard to just be in the moment without thinking about where it's going. You're either driven toward pleasure and can't slow down to explore other touch or to linger where you are, or you're feeling bad that you don't seem to be hitting the goal or expectation. You feel bad that it isn't working again. You're either anticipating (or worried about) what happens after the exercise, instead of being in the present with the experience you're having.

BREAKTHROUGH: LETTING GO OF THE GOAL

You let go of the idea that anything is *supposed* to happen for either you or your partner. You are relieved of the burden to perform. If you (or your partner) are getting aroused, you can still be in the moment without pushing or driving toward anything else. You don't worry about what comes next. You don't get ahead of yourself, anticipating what comes next or what you'll do after the exercise.

Phase 5—Learning to Be Present

Our minds are busy creatures. You can get so consumed with thoughts, ideas and stories that you are totally unaware of what is going on around you, disconnected from the present moment and the actual person you are with.

You may find it hard to turn off your mind from constantly running through your to-do list or overanalyzing worries about life and work. Thoughts of planning, evaluating, and strategizing about what you will be doing next are swirling around in your mind like a whirlpool. It may be hard to switch gears and put those concerns aside to show up and be present with your partner. If your mind is busy and you are "all in your head," you may have a hard time "getting into your body"—where you can be aware of your physical self, feel and focus on sensation, and connect with touch and stimulation in a way that allows you to get aroused and interested in sex.

Your mind may also be busy with self-conscious and self-critical thoughts. Worry about your body, your sexual performance, or the state of your relationship can also get in the way of you having a good time in sex. Your expectations about sex—for you, your partner, and your encounter as a whole—can start to consume you. And your judgments about how you're doing compared to those expectations can be another layer of mental busywork that gets in the way of sexual enjoyment. If you or your partner is distracted or worried during sex, it can become that much harder to enjoy it (giving you one more thing to worry about). And as that continues to grow and build, you will likely find your interest in sex declining.

Sex is enhanced when you can relax and be fully engaged in each moment. Stress, anxiety, fears, and distractions diminish your access to pleasure and connection with your partner and what you are doing together. It's important to learn to relax, slow down, and just take in the breadth of your experience. This includes the subtlety of the physical sensations you are having in your whole body, the thoughts and feelings you are having while doing it, and the awareness of your partner. You will increase your sexual satisfaction if you learn to minimize those things that pull you out of your experience.

Learning to slow down and pay attention is a good skill to have in all areas of life, and it is very important for good sex and for a sense of connection with your partner. Can you tell what your body is feeling? Can you feel your sensations? Are you aware of the emotions you are having? Can you identify your thoughts and recognize they are nothing more than that? Can you just be? Can you allow yourself and your partner to temporarily leave reality behind?

I recommend developing a mindfulness practice in your life. Whether you learn to meditate or develop the habit of sitting quietly and just noticing what is happening for you, in your mind, body, and emotions, you can get better at being present and aware of each moment.

There are several practices you can do together with your partner, as well. One tool is eye gazing, done for 5 to 10 minutes at a time. Sit in chairs, facing each other. Adjust the distance between your chairs so your eyes can focus on each other. Sit with your feet flat on the floor and relax. Hold your gaze on your partner's left eye (to your right). Let yourself just be in this experience; there is no need to mask what you're thinking or feeling. Notice how your body feels, what emotions come up, and what sensory experiences you have. Let go of any judgment you have about what's happening for you or what might seem to be happening for your partner. This is a good practice for letting yourself be seen, as well as just being in the moment.

Once you have some comfort holding each other's gazes, you can add an element of synchronizing your breathing. Begin by breathing in and out at the same time, so that you both draw breath in together. Once you've aligned your breathing together, switch to alternate breathing: when your partner breathes in, you breathe out, and vice versa. Keep your body relaxed and your breathing slow.

Using the Receiver Exercise— Learning to be present

You and your partner can use the exercise to practice being present. Because you are taking time out of real life to do an exercise, you can slow down. You are taking one role at a time, and that gives you the chance to notice everything going on with you—thoughts, feelings, sensations. As you pay attention to these things, you will grow adept at tuning in and being *in* your experience. The exercise is a place to practice showing up with whatever you've got, learning to relax and bring yourself to the moment. Settling your brain down is an important step before you can fully participate in the exercise and get the most from it. Don't worry if it takes time to be able to show up and just be present in the exercise.

PITFALL 1: BEING STEEPED IN SELF-CRITICISM
AND/OR SELF-CONSCIOUSNESS

You may spend your turn feeling bad that you don't know what you want. Or you might feel bad about whatever it is you do want. If you believe you should want sexual touch, but don't, you may not allow yourself to ask for or enjoy other kinds of touch that you would like. If you want sexual touch, but your partner is struggling with that, you may feel bad about that the whole time instead of enjoying what you're being given. You may judge your progress or your struggles. You may feel self-conscious or hateful about your body. You may spend the whole 10 minutes in negative thought that gets in the way of you enjoying the touch you're getting.

BREAKTHROUGH 1: STOPPING THE SELF-TALK/CRITICISM

Your critical inner voice shuts up. You let go of the self-doubt. You stop judging your body, your thoughts, your desires. You let yourself just be in the moment with what is and stop holding yourself up to some standard or expectation. You can't fail this. You're okay knowing it is what it is, that this is one experience of many. You finally feel good about yourself as a sexual person, wanting what you want, responding however you respond.

PITFALL 2: BEING STUCK IN YOUR HEAD, DISTRACTED

You can't stop thinking about the chores that need doing or what's going on at work. You're a list maker, and the list is too long to take time out to be intimate. You've always lived in your head and never sit still for long to connect with your body or your sensations. You analyze everything, so you live (at least) one step removed from your experience in the world. The idea of taking 10 minutes to just be—without thinking about it and without knowing what's going to happen—doesn't sound inviting.

BREAKTHROUGH 2: SETTLING DOWN YOUR MIND

You learn to quiet your mind and let go of the thoughts that still show up. You find a peace and relaxation you didn't know before. You've learned to leave your to-do list at the door and that you can pick it back up once you're ready. You've also learned to let work stay at work and to let some chores go undone (or at least wait until later). You've slowed down a little and found you are more productive when you aren't so harried.

Phase 6—Being Okay With No

It's important that each of you take care of yourselves in your relationship in general, and it is particularly important in your sex life. As I discussed in Chapter 4, each of you must figure out when you *need* to say no. That's the foundation of trust in a sex life, knowing that your partner will safeguard themselves and is choosing to participate sexually with you. You each need the ability to discern what is good for you and what is bad, and you need the skill to say no when that's appropriate. Likewise, you need the ability to hear no when your partner is taking care of themselves and recognize no as a good thing in that situation.

Life gives you plenty of opportunity to practice with no. Think about how you deal with no on a regular basis. Are you one of those people who take on way too much? Do you hate to disappoint people? Do you give so much of yourself that there's nothing left for you (or your relationship) when the week is over? You can start learning to say no right now, in all the various areas of your life. You can set limits at work, with friends, and with family. You can start with small things and work up to bigger ones. Watch yourself and see what you find out about what makes you say yes when you shouldn't. See if you can gradually start to have some boundaries.

Likewise, you should pay attention to how you handle other people saying no to you. How often do you take it personally? To what degree do you feel entitled to have your wants met? Do you avoid asking for things so that you can avoid hearing a no? Maybe you're one of those people who only hint at what they want so you don't have to hear a direct denial. Or perhaps you manipulate situations toward your desired outcome, so there's no chance for the other person to be clear about your request and to agree with it or not. If you get better about being direct about your desires and ask to have your wants and needs met, you'll end up with more opportunity to deal with hearing no. Asking for what you want and risking denial will be a challenge, but it is a crucial skill in building a successful relationship and sex life.

Using the Receiver Exercise— Being Okay With No

The exercise will give you plenty of practice discerning when you need to say no and then practice in both saying and hearing a refusal. You will gain the trust that your partner will take care of themselves. They'll get that chance repeatedly while using the exercise. When one of you says no, the instruction is to just move on to something else. It will get easier to hear a no while continuing to feel connected and keeping the encounter going.

PITFALL 1: STRUGGLING TO SAY NO APPROPRIATELY

You say no to their request and feel bad about it. You see the look on their face and take it on. Or you know them well enough to know they'll be disappointed, and you struggle with that. You're so worried about them that taking care of yourself seems like a problem.

You don't say no when you should and have a bad experience. You sacrifice yourself because you have this idea that they won't be okay. Or you're so used to doing that, it's hard to distinguish when you need to say no. You struggle to take care of yourself.

You say no when you didn't need to. You're so used to setting limits and shutting things down that you don't take on the work of getting out of your comfort zone. You may have so much resentment or hard feelings that it's hard to let that go and engage with the work of opening your heart and challenging yourself.

BREAKTHROUGH 1: LEARNING TO TAKE CARE OF YOURSELF

You know what it feels like to need to say no. You know yourself well enough to know what a negative experience for you will be. You feel good about taking care of yourself, and you do it easily and without guilt. You don't sacrifice yourself. This allows you to accept your partner's desires more easily. You don't feel threatened or pressured since you know you ultimately get to decide.

You move into discomfort with intention (also known as getting out of your comfort zone). You are willing to challenge yourself to learn new things and develop new capacity. You are willing to feel anxious and work through it. You walk into challenges because you know it is good for you. You master your own emotional state and anxiety. You are willing to push yourself just enough to be useful and productive. You've moved past saying no as a knee-jerk reaction.

PITFALL 2: A PROBLEM HEARING NO

If your partner needs to say no to something, that impacts your experience. It triggers all the negative feelings that have built up around your sex life. You feel rejected and sad. You feel like you were wrong to ask for what you did, and you may determine to rein it in the next time. You believe they aren't taking the exercise or their self-confrontation seriously or really trying. You may sulk, quit, or only go through the motions for the rest of your turn, unable to continue being focused on what feels good and enjoying it.

BREAKTHROUGH 2: CELEBRATING HEARING NO

You come to realize that your partner saying no is a good thing; it means they are taking care of themselves. You move on easily to another request and can enjoy that fully. You have a wealth of things that can feel good, and one can replace another without a problem. You ask for exactly what you want without concern about whether your partner will say no or not, knowing that you will be fine if they can't do it.

Phase 7—Being Selfish

Most people are raised to believe that selfishness is bad. And it certainly can be. There are plenty of people who manage to get their orgasm regardless of whether they connect with or think about their partner, but that is not a wholesome selfishness. That is bred of insecurity and smallness. I am talking about being selfish in a good way. I am talking about being able to take pleasure, ask for what you want, and allow yourself to soak up pleasure with abandon. This kind of selfishness is crucial to great sex. Having the strength to want and receive is a powerful thing. Being able to *relish* your experience, *dive* into sensation, and *luxuriate* in sex brings passion and dimension to your sexual encounters. This ability enhances not only your own enjoyment, but also your partner's. It is attractive to want! You are a much more compelling sex partner when you thoroughly enjoy yourself.

But this selfishness is hard to do when you have been raised to be a people pleaser. Many of you were brought up and trained to always be looking for ways to be of service, keep the peace, be easygoing, and roll with the punches. As a people pleaser, you may take pride in your ability to accommodate and not need too much. Your friends appreciate your easygoing attitude, and you may find yourself coasting through life without much conflict.

And yet, like so much in life, this comes with a cost. If you focus only on pleasing others, you may not know what *you* want or have any sense of how to figure that out. You may have devoted so much time and energy figuring out what others wanted and trying to give them those things that you never took the time to tune in and see what *you* would choose.

Over time, some of you have learned to bury your desires because it was clear early on you weren't going to get them met anyway. They may be buried so deeply by now that you can't seem to find them. But somewhere inside of you there are things you want. And over time, if you ignore those wants and desires, a feeling starts to smolder. It may be unhappiness. Or resentment. Or maybe just a worrying feeling of being unsettled. But something simply isn't right.

At some point, going along with what others want becomes a problem. Some of you will hit a wall, suddenly, and can't go along anymore. Others get to this place more gradually, with a consistently growing and gnawing sense of dissatisfaction and unease. In whatever way you get there, once you do, there is no turning back. Your desires will make it to the surface one way or another. The question is, are you going to wait for them to explode on their own? Or will you proactively start looking for them now?

There is another cost to always being the one who accommodates: your partner never gets the opportunity to give to you. There is something profound in being able to please someone else. If you don't give your partner the opportunity, you are depriving them of that experience. When in Thailand many years ago, I was watching the Buddhist monks begging for rice among the crowd. In talking to my tour guide, I became intrigued when he explained that they were providing a service: offering a gift of the opportunity to give. This applies to all of us. Allowing yourself to want (and allowing your partner to give by fulfilling those wants) is a critical part of a good relationship—and good sex.

A balanced relationship is key to a great sex life. You need to be able to think about yourself in addition to thinking about your partner. In great sex, there is a dynamic of being both selfish and giving. If you or your partner only has sex for the *other* person's pleasure, or if you've only had sex in the way that works for the other person, you are out of balance. It is not sustainable to keep pouring from a cup that doesn't get filled. Eventually, it feels draining at the least, and toxic at the worst. Once sex starts to feel negative, sex is going to suffer unless you step up and bring your own wants into the equation. It's important to be able to be selfish.

Having the strength to access your desire and then act from that place opens sex up and creates a more fulfilling experience for both people. Letting your partner give to you, as well as share in and enjoy your pleasure, can make their experience better. Sex starts to get hollow if it's always about one person's enjoyment, even if that one person is you. Ideally, you create a flow where you each get a chance to think about yourself and receive.

To practice being selfish in your life, you can use the same strategies I suggested in the stage where you were accessing desire. Think about yourself and ask for what you want. Let yourself focus on what would make you happy. Rely on your partner to take care of himself or herself and to speak up if they have a problem. Remember, you don't have to take care of them. See what it's like to indulge yourself.

Using the Receiver Exercise— Being Selfish

The zeal of selfishness takes openness and confidence as well as a strong alliance with your partner. You are exposed in sexual desire. That's why it takes practice and growth. You can use the Giver/Receiver Exercise to stretch the limits of your pleasure and your ability to revel in it. You can ask for exactly what you want, and you can practice taking the space to think only about what would feel best, letting your partner set the limits they need in order to participate with you in a healthy way. Watch what happens as you explore positive selfishness!

PITFALL: INABILITY TO PUT YOURSELF FIRST

It's hard for you to think about yourself. You may have spent your life focused on the pleasure of the person you're with, or you may have more recently decided that you need to worry more about your partner.

You worry that your partner won't like your choice, so you censor. If you believe that the touch should (or shouldn't) be sexual, you limit your choices to those expectations instead of really tuning in to see what you want in that moment. Or you ask for what you want, but you watch your partner for their reactions (their comfort) and gauge from there. You spend the whole time wondering if they are okay, instead of being in your own experience.

BREAKTHROUGH: GIVING YOURSELF PERMISSION TO BE SELFISH

You can think about yourself, to be selfish in a good way. You take up space and let yourself have a turn. You allow yourself full access to your desires, and you relish receiving that touch. You trust your partner will take care of himself or herself, freeing you to let go of all those cares and savor the experience. You feel unburdened, free, and expansive. It feels good!

Phase 8—Giving

Being selfish in sex needs to be balanced with allowing your partner to do the same, putting you in the role as the one who gives what the other wants or allows them to take their own pleasure. You don't have to balance this equally every time you have sex, but there should be a good balance overall. Create the space for your partner to desire and soak in their own pleasure. Be an active participant in inviting and responding to their selfishness.

You may have a partner who isn't able to enjoy sex fully. Perhaps they are shut down, repressed, ashamed, or self-conscious. This tones down sex, bringing the potential vibrancy of pleasure down to shades of beige. Working with your partner to explore their desires, their fullness, and their ability to abandon themselves to pleasure will pay off for both of you. This focus on them takes being able to set your needs aside and give.

You can work on giving in your day-to-day life. Make space for your partner to have their wants and needs met. Set yourself aside, sometimes, to fully get on board with them. Notice how often you shut them down to pursue your own agenda. How often do you expect to get what you want while ignoring or minimizing what would make your partner happy? How often do you expect them to cater to your wishes, but you don't reciprocate?

Using the Receiver Exercise—Giving

You can use the Giver/Receiver Exercise to immerse yourself in the role of Giver. After taking care of the boundaries you need, you can work to open your heart to *want* to give the pleasure your partner is requesting. You can follow directions carefully, tuning into their body language and signals, as well as their words. Invite them into that space; let them know there is room for their pleasure and desires. See what unfolds when you try it!

PITFALL 1: DIFFICULTY HEARING DIRECTION

You feel like you should know what they want already. You feel like the things you're learning now show you've been doing it wrong all along. You feel criticized. You feel stubborn; you struggle to do things when people tell you to. You feel an urge to withhold what's being asked. Or you struggle to want to do it well since it's their idea.

BREAKTHROUGH 1: LOVING DIRECTION

The pressure is off. You don't have to know what they want. You don't need to be an expert or impress them. You just follow directions. It's freeing to know they are getting what they want because it's up to them to ask for it. You feel the burden that you are responsible for their pleasure has lifted. You are a partner in it, allowing you to relax and simply put yourself into doing what they describe.

PITFALL 2: NOT LIKING WHAT YOUR PARTNER CHOOSES

Sometimes, your partner will express a desire for something that you don't like. You struggle with the line between needing to say no and just wanting to. You're anxious or turned off. It's not what you want, so it's hard to do it, and it's certainly hard to want to do it. It's difficult to stay present. You're thinking about how you feel about it instead of being present with it. You may feel like you should like it and thus get into self-criticism. Or you worry what all this means.

BREAKTHROUGH 2: ENJOYMENT OF PLEASING THEM

You want to please them. You love being able to give. You love seeing your partner happy. You're learning things about what they like, and you're learning to like some of the things that please them. You're moving through any discomfort you have with certain acts and expanding the repertoire of touch and sensation.

PITFALL 3: JUDGING YOUR PARTNER

You may judge your partner for their choice. You may feel they should be asking for sexual touch and are hurt or annoyed that they aren't. You feel like they aren't doing the exercise correctly, or they aren't pushing their boundaries. Or you think they shouldn't ask for something sexual, and you think they're pushing *your* boundaries. Judgment gets in the way of you just being in the experience, and you get annoyed or frustrated or disappointed.

BREAKTHROUGH 3: LETTING GO OF JUDGMENT

You let go of the idea that your partner is supposed to want anything specific. You value what they ask for because it is exactly what they want in that moment. You let go of any ideas that their requests should be sexual—or that they shouldn't be. You give your partner the freedom they need.

Phase 9—Exploring Eroticism

Early in a relationship, there is often plenty to get excited about. The two of you generally have enough overlap in your sexual interests to find at least some room to play. But over time, you may have gotten into a sexual rut. Throughout a relationship, you tend to take anything off the table that makes either of you uncomfortable. Unfortunately, you may have ways of being sexually intimate that you really like or are interested in that were taken off the menu in those early days when everything was new and exciting. Being careful to not make your partner uncomfortable, you may have gotten to a place now where you feel like you're really missing something. It's also common to play it safe with your partner and not make *yourself* uncomfortable. You don't reveal too much about what really turns you on.

It's been said that the brain is the biggest sex organ, so if you're not using yours, you're missing out. The brain is what adds meaning and psychological depth to what you're doing. The brain is what turns words, gestures, and acts into erotic stimuli. If you leave out eroticism, you risk dulling your sexual experience.

You each have an eroticism that is uniquely yours. There are specific things that turn you on. And it's not just the specific physical acts but the meaning of those acts (the energetics around them) that make them exciting. There can be themes of power, romanticism, prohibition, danger, mystery, presence, and more that underlie what really "flips your switch." Your eroticism is revealed in your sexual preferences, your fantasies, and your reactions to erotic media, both written and visual. If you aren't clear about your own eroticism, you can explore fantasies and erotica to see where it leads you.

There is a lot of fuel in your eroticism; it has power. And if you've been going through your sex life without tapping into what is erotic for each of you, you're not maximizing your interest and arousal. If sex is seeming stale and boring, exploring eroticism is one powerful way to breathe new life into it.

Of course, a lot of people don't ever get to this level of exploration because it's very intimate to share your eroticism with your partner, and that can be scary. You may not have ever thought about what's hot to you, never explored this at all, so you don't know where to start. Or if you do know, you may not know how to share it with someone who may or may not accept it. You may not want to rock the boat or risk the anxiety of showing someone else this side of you.

Now that you have shifted from avoiding sex to actively engaging with your partner to change the dynamics, and you've worked through the other phases of this process, you can explore eroticism together. Making sex erotic is powerful fuel for sexual interest and arousal.

Beginning to explore your own eroticism with your partner can open new levels of intimacy and intensity. This is not for the faint of heart; it can feel very risky to show this side of your sexual self. You may be ashamed of your sexual turn-ons, and you don't know until you share them whether or not your partner will embrace them. Coming to terms with your eroticism and making room for it in the conversation with your partner, whether or not you will incorporate it into your sex life, can take some time and patience.

The first step, once you've got some idea of what turns you on and what is salient in your eroticism, is to imagine how you can bring that about with your partner. What would you have to ask your partner to do to explore your deepest erotic desires? Then you can discuss this with them. I recommend sharing scenes with each other that you each find hot. Go into this with the agreement that you won't criticize each other. Try to keep curiosity and openness about what you each find to be a turn on. You are not, at this point, talking about doing anything with this information; you are just learning about each other. You can share scenes from written erotica, movies or TV shows, or from visual erotica, including pornography, if you wish. You can point out which part(s) of the scene are fundamental to your response to it—which parts are hot and which parts don't matter or get erased in your mind, so you can focus on what turns you on. Sharing more than one scene allows both of you to see the basic theme of what underlies your unique eroticism.

The next step might be to share your actual sexual fantasies. Knowing that your partner might not respond especially well to your ideas, agree to the same respect and lack of criticism as when you shared other people's scenes. Since these are created in your mind, they only include elements that work for you. There are no off-putting elements that you must overlook, as there often are in porn or other media. After all, why add elements to a fantasy that would make it worse? This means it's more personal, too, since your fantasies are pure erotic material that reveal your core erotic nature. When you let your partner see this level of detail about what turns you on, you are showing them extremely personal information about you and your essence.

Through this exploration with your partner, you're going to get an idea of where you overlap in eroticism and where you don't. It is my belief that no two people choose each other if there isn't at least some overlap in what they find erotic. It's not a problem if you don't find the exact same things arousing. You'll want to find the overlap and start there. Then you can start to explore those things that are outside your comfort zone, but that you might be willing to entertain because it's pleasing to your partner. And vice versa.

The places where you overlap are easy to use and play with. Whether you decide to *do* some of the things that turn either of you on (whether acting out a whole scene or just playing with parts of it), or you harness the erotic energy by just talking about or imagining it, you can start to incorporate the energy right away. Some of the erotic ideas that don't overlap can still be part of your sex life. You can use some of them, even though it's out of your comfort zone. Or maybe you're willing to role play or imagine some of the things that excite your partner even though it doesn't excite you. Sometimes you can build ways to play that use elements from each of your fantasies, finding how they can go together in a way that works. Other erotic elements may just be off the table in your relationship (giving you another opportunity to practice saying or hearing no). In that case, those themes can be explored and enjoyed in solo sex.

Using the Receiver Exercise—Exploring eroticism

You can use the Giver/Receiver Exercise to explore eroticism once you have made good progress with all the other phases of this process. Because you are directing your partner, in exquisite detail, about what you want, you can capture elements of your eroticism in your requests. Eroticism is more about *how* things are done, and sometimes less about *what* things are done. See what it's like to add this dimension to what you describe to your partner when it's your turn to receive.

PITFALL 1: INABILITY TO PUT YOUR EROTIC DESIRES INTO WORDS

You don't know how to describe what you want. There's something you want to feel, but it's vague to you and hard to name. You feel embarrassed about what you like, so it's hard for you to be clear about the details that really make the experience powerful for you. You worry that your partner won't react well or will judge you for your desires.

BREAKTHROUGH 1: FINDING A WAY TO COMMUNICATE WITH YOUR PARTNER, SO THEY CAN MEET YOUR DESIRES, AS THEY ARE ABLE

You use the ideas above, about sharing erotic media and fantasies, outside of the exercise time to help communicate the subtlety of what you want. You are open with your partner about which parts are essential to your arousal. You validate your own desires and tolerate any judgment or ambivalence from your partner. You develop some language to help you describe exactly what you want. You have experiences that tap into your erotic mind and infuse your sex life with new energy.

PITFALL 2: NOT ENJOYING THE SAME EROTIC SCENES THAT YOUR PARTNER DOES, AND IT SEEMS TO GO BADLY

You can't enjoy your turn if your partner isn't into it. You worry about how they're feeling instead of allowing yourself your pleasure. You hold back what you really want since you know (or suspect) that it isn't such a turn on for them. Or you push hard for what you want, trying to pressure your partner into participating in something they really don't like. When the Giver, you fail to discern when you need to say no and end up having a negative experience. Or you let your discomfort with your partner's requests keep you from trying to play in that space with them and expanding your sexual repertoire.

BREAKTHROUGH 2: WORKING WITH YOUR OVERLAP AS WELL AS PLAYING WITHIN BOUNDARIES THAT MAKE IT A POSITIVE EXPERIENCE

You and your partner have had a lot of discussion and exploration about what makes sex erotic to each of you. You get adept at knowing what is a hard no for you and what you can try to explore (and even enjoy). You make your requests clear, and you don't push your partner beyond their appropriate boundaries.

Try a version of the exercise focused on taking and allowing pleasure.

Once you have fully explored the Giver/Receiver Exercise, you may want to use the counterpart: the Taker/Allower version of the exercise. The person doing the touching is in charge—they are taking pleasure and the other allows it. Occasionally, people may choose to start with this one. The consent built into this exercise is important (especially if one of you has had abuse, trauma, or assault in the past). Doing this exercise can be a healing way to proceed, though I think doing the original Giver/Receiver Exercise first helps you develop the communication you need to be successful with this variation. Either way, you can use the Taker/Allower exercise to proceed through the same 9 phases described earlier.

The same rules apply for this exercise as with the Giver/Receiver Exercise, but the directions and jobs are slightly different. In this case, it is the Taker that is in charge. The Taker is to think about how they would touch the Allower *for their own pleasure.* They ask for consent to do that specific thing, and then touch the Allower in that way. Unlike much of the touch people provide their partners, this exercise asks the Taker to think about themselves and what they would enjoy doing, for their own sensory pleasure, what sensual or sensory experience they would like to have with their partner's body.

It is crucial for the Taker to ask for consent. Let the Allower know specifically what you want to do—where you want to touch and how. Get explicit verbal consent before proceeding. Ask again every time you want to change what you are doing. The Allower has the same job of saying no when they *need* to say no, and consciously choosing to step into the work of growth when they just *want* to say no.

You take the same 10-minute turns as with the Giver/Receiver Exercise, with the same jobs to pay attention to during your roles.

———

Change happens experientially. You need to practice thinking and behaving differently to transform your sex life. This chapter is all about how to put these ideas into physical practice with your partner. The exercises give you the framework for change; the phases give you the areas of focus to change. By the end of the process, however long that takes, you and your partner can discover freedom and ease in your sexual relationship.

Let's revisit our four example couples one last time. You'll get to hear about their experiences using the exercise and what kinds of challenges and breakthroughs they had in various stages of learning. You will see that by the end of the process, they have transformed their sex lives and are enjoying each other again. The sense of hopelessness they had at the beginning of the book now seems like a distant memory. That is what I want for you, too.

Carol and Todd

Carol:

When they start using the exercise to access desire, Carol struggles with knowing what to ask for after her mastectomy. Her breasts had always been sexually sensitive and pleasing. Now she has a flat chest and scars. She feels weird when she and Todd both avoid her chest area, but neither of them knows how to act now. She is also grieving the loss of her breasts and their sexual pleasure every time they have sex. She uses the exercise to gently explore her new body, and to invite Todd to touch her.

Carol gradually makes peace with her body through the process. She and Todd explore touch to her chest, and while it isn't sexually arousing anymore, she can appreciate the touch on her skin. It allows them both to get comfortable with her new look and her scars. Her chest feels like part of her body again. And once they've gotten over that hurdle, she uses her turns as the receiver in the exercise for touch that is sexually arousing. The absence of her breasts no longer overshadows their sexual encounters.

As the Giver, Carol struggles at first to touch and stimulate his penis. She'd spent her life avoiding it, and she feels nervous and queasy whenever she starts. It gets easier the more she does it, and she isn't thinking about it as much now. Early on, she continues to measure herself by the state of Todd's erection. She keeps wanting and expecting Todd to get hard if he gets stimulation to his penis, and now that she's providing that, she feels disappointed if it doesn't result in an erection. Anything else feels like a failure. She doubts herself and her sexual abilities, but she also struggles to find any meaning in interacting sexually with him when he doesn't get an erection. She has a hard time being present as the Giver since she feels like nothing really counts until he is physically aroused. She sometimes even finds herself getting bored. She has to push herself to tune into him and let him decide what he wants and what he finds pleasurable.

Eventually, Carol settles down and gives up worrying about whether Todd will get hard or not. It takes some time to accept that this seems to be a permanent change due to age. She allows herself to feel sad for the change, but then she can be present with whatever is happening. As Todd accepts this, too, and begins to explore his whole body, she can show up and really participate with him in the experience. She learns to let go of the idea that his erection determines her desirability, and she feels much lighter once she does that. She finds she enjoys touching him a lot. It doesn't have the heat or intensity of the sex they used to have, but there is a sweetness and intimacy in their exploration that is powerful. Because he still feels pleasure at the touch of his penis, hard or not, she is able to focus on his pleasure and not on the result.

Todd:

Todd recognizes that there are things about his life with Carol that he wants to change and that he never felt like he could address with her due to his own fear. He starts some conversations, clumsily at first, to learn to talk about the hard things. He gets better with practice, and he finds that for the most part Carol is interested in hearing from him and wants to make the changes he's requesting.

One of the first things he brings up is the lack of touch she gives him during sex. It's a stretch for him to have a difficult conversation at all, but especially one about his sexual pleasure since it will likely trigger her insecurities. He feels anxious as he starts the conversation, but he manages to hold himself together and make his points. Although she gets defensive at first, he sticks with it. His grounded response helps her see that this means a lot to him, and she settles herself down to finish the talk.

Todd still feels like he should get aroused with touch, and he will push for that, even though he is physically unable to get an erection some of the time. Sometimes, he'll sneak a pill before the exercise, so he will seem to succeed. That focus on a goal keeps him from using the exercise to explore what might be pleasing to him. Once he admits to Carol that he is using a pill and is still goal-oriented, he can give that up and just let things happen.

Todd finds pleasure after he relaxes about getting an erection. It takes a while, but he begins to ask for touch all over his body. He finds that he really likes being stroked gently all down his arms and legs. He has a much more sensual experience than he'd ever allowed himself while his penis was "working." He eventually instructs Carol to touch his penis, too, and can enjoy the sensation he has even if he doesn't become fully erect (although that happens sometimes). He feels much more at peace with himself after this.

What they find at the end of this process is that they are more able to relax and enjoy sex than they have ever been. They no longer focus on a goal, they each have found things that are pleasurable, and they work together to make sure they get what they want out of each sexual encounter they have. Sometimes they have intercourse, and other times they explore pleasure in the other ways they've discovered. They are willing to address their concerns and frustrations with each other, and they've built the skills to solve problems, not just fight about them. They have remained active and engaged with each other and are enjoying the beginning of their retirement.

Beth and Yara

Yara:

Yara feels self-critical early in the exercise. She struggles with her own baggage about feeling dirty for being a sexual person. She also feels like she is bad or wrong for wanting rougher and faster touch, especially compared to Beth. At first, she doesn't ask for what she really wants because she can't let go of these thoughts. It takes time for her to slowly reveal what she really wants and to struggle with the emotions that her desires bring up.

Yara overcomes her self-criticism as she does the exercise more. Over time, she finds a peace with her sexual self and can accept her desires as valid and good. She recognizes the internal voices of her parents, and she rejects them. She learns to replace that self-talk with something more positive. When she does, she starts to feel empowered about her sexuality instead of ashamed. This is a tipping point for her, allowing her to open up more about what she wants and enjoy getting it.

Yara also starts to speak up around the house. She no longer avoids making some plans for herself with friends when Beth has to work late. She realizes how much she'd held herself back out of fear of Beth's jealousy and disappointment. When Beth reverts to trying to make her feel bad, she is grounded and clear and able to respectfully call Beth out for that.

Beth:

Beth struggles to be present in the exercise. Part of the reason she's been avoiding sex is because she has such a hard time getting aroused. Her mind is always spinning with thoughts of her changed body, as well as with life's distractions. She can't change gears quickly, so she thinks she can't change gears at all. She feels overwhelmed with everything that needs to get done. She has figured that her sex life with Yara can just wait until life gets simpler. The problem is, life doesn't get simpler, and so their intimate connection had been disintegrating.

It takes Beth many repetitions of the exercise before she stops fighting her mind and just relaxes. She gives up expectations that it should be easy and resigns herself to accept whatever happens. For a while, she keeps thinking about all the things she should be doing or how her body should be working, but that lessens over time. It's nice to get a massage, and it helps her relax and feel good. She begins to look forward to the exercise since she can get some relief and some pleasure. Once she allows herself to receive massage and sees that Yara is happy to make her feel good, she warms to her touch. She gets more engaged in her turns as Giver, too.

As they do the exercise in a more sexual way, Beth struggles with not knowing what she wants. It is a big deal for her to start to explore how she might want to be touched, to let Yara see her as unsure and tentative. With practice, Beth does learn what she wants. Her body is different now. She needs slower and more gentle touch, but she finds that she still responds to and enjoys it. She explores more of her body than she used to use in sex and learns new things about what will please her.

Both in real life and as the Giver during the exercise, Beth struggles with feelings of judgment about Yara's desires. Yara wants more aggressive and passionate touch, and Beth vilifies that in her mind since she no longer responds to that style of sex herself. She used to, and she feels bad about the change. So, for a while, she turns her disappointment about her own sexual response into judging Yara for what she wants.

Beth ends up letting go of her judgment about Yara wanting more vigorous interaction as she makes peace with the changes in her own sexuality. She accepts that what Yara wants is about Yara, and each of them can like what they like. She stops feeling like she should match Yara or must keep up somehow, and she gets into the role of giving Yara what she desires.

At the end of the process, Yara and Beth have open communication about what each of them is feeling. They have explored what arouses each of them sexually and integrated that into ways to have sex that they both like. When there are problems, they are more able to address what's really going on between them and will bring up issues in a timely manner. They hold each other accountable, and they each can accept feedback and admit when they've slipped back into old patterns. They are having more fun together, spending evenings together and adopting new habits like eating together at the table without any devices on. They no longer avoid sex.

Jenny and Rich

Jenny:

Jenny says no a lot at first, protective of herself and still struggling to relinquish the power she has over sex. She's been saying no to sex for quite some time, and even though she hesitantly agrees to do the exercise, she doesn't agree to do much within it. Once she takes herself on about how she is using the control that comes with being the lower desire partner, she overcompensates and starts to say yes to everything, trying to give it a go. Sometimes that backfires, since she has such a negative response to being sexual with Rich when she isn't feeling sexual herself. She struggles to discern the line between needing to say no and just wanting to.

This gets easier with practice. She gets adept at challenging herself and stepping into acts or mental spaces that make her uncomfortable, but she will also speak up when it feels a "certain kind of bad." She learns to use her no to really take care of herself instead of to control Rich. Because she gets better at no, her yes means yes. She feels tremendous strength and empowerment in mastering taking care of herself in a healthy way.

As the Giver, sometimes Jenny doesn't like what Rich wants. She hasn't yet learned to be a fan of oral sex, and sometimes he will ask to feel her mouth on his penis. Given that she is also fighting her own resistance to working on sex at all, she has a hard time getting to a place where she is willing to do what he wants. She is largely focused on her past dislike of the act instead of just seeing what it is like in the moment.

This, too, gets better with time. It takes a while, but she starts to expand her ability to do what someone else wants from a healthy and willing place. She learns to do things that she doesn't necessarily enjoy and still feel empowered. This is a major change in her mindset, and she's on her way to having a different relationship with power and control. She still isn't loving oral sex, but she's developing a comfort with it and no longer has a negative response to the request.

Rich:

When they start doing the exercise, Rich feels rejected whenever Jenny says no. It doesn't help that she's been saying no to sex for quite a while, and he is used to feeling rejected. Each time she sets a boundary, he spirals into a negative cycle, feeling more hopeless about their sex life. He struggles to see the exercise as just one experience that allows them to grow.

With practice and with conversation between them, Rich overcomes his sense of rejection when Jenny takes care of herself by setting limits. It helps him to see that Jenny is confronting herself about her use of power in turning him down for sex. He can tell she is genuinely saying yes now, different than when she used to just go along with sex. That helps him experience her saying no as an important step in her growth. He stops making her choices about him and realizes it is about her. This shift helps his mood, and he stops getting depressed and hopeless as they hit bumps in the process.

Rich makes a major change in how he's been dealing with the house and the kids. Once he recognized that he was effectively taking out his frustration with Jenny on the children, he makes a distinct change and starts to engage with them. He steps into more responsibility at home and spends more time supporting and interacting with the kids.

Jenny and Rich are in a much better place after this process. Jenny has decided to start individual therapy to deal with the impact of her family and to continue the growth she's experiencing in discovering her voice, her desires, and her power. She is more able to change her mindset and show up for sex from a place of openness. She's learning more about what she wants sexually, and she's putting that into words. She's prioritizing time with Rich, whether it's for a date night or an intimate encounter. She will absolutely say no to things when she needs to, but she's got an entirely new ability to say yes and mean it. Rich has mostly gotten over his tendency to take her desire (or lack thereof) personally. He manages his emotions and rarely gets sullen or anxious now in response to their sex life. He's become a much more attentive lover and partner. They are talking openly about sex, parenting, household responsibilities, and how they feel about those topics.

Tom and Grant

Tom and Grant quickly see that they use the joking, indirect approach that they take to sex with the exercise as well. They make wisecracks about the exercise. They admit that they feel awkward and silly, and it is easier to joke it off than address it. After naming that, they then push themselves to jump in and do it. Their joking subsides after that, and the exercise gets easier after they do it the first time.

Tom:

Tom has a hard time asking Grant for anything sexual. His previous partners had always taken charge, so he's never had to put his desires into words. He hasn't gotten exactly what he wanted before, but that was okay since he didn't have to speak up. He does have some ideas about what pleases him, but it is like pulling teeth to get him to talk about it. Grant is completely open to hearing from Tom, but it takes some time before Tom can say what he wants. It is a gradual process, but he gets better about being specific in describing what would feel best to him. Since he has never talked about sex, it is slow going. But the payoff is immense, since he really starts to enjoy what he is getting. He starts to talk about what he wants outside of the exercise, too, and that makes a huge difference in their sex (and everyday) life.

At first when they do the exercise, Tom spends most of his turns aware of, and nervous about, how Grant is experiencing what is happening. Even though he is supposed to be focused on his own pleasure, he can't enjoy it if Grant doesn't seem happy. And even when he does, Tom worries about what Grant is really thinking.

Tom finds incredible freedom once he starts thinking about himself. After he gives himself permission to not worry about Grant, letting Grant take care of himself, Tom completely relaxes in the exercise and has a great time. It happens suddenly for him, once he just decides he can be "selfish." He asks for all kinds of things he enjoys, and he lets himself completely enjoy it. He explores a lot of touch and stimulation and learns more about what he likes. He also starts to release the shame he's felt about his sexual orientation. He lets go of a huge burden, and his anxiety evaporates.

Tom gets much better at handling conflict between them. He doesn't joke so much anymore, and he even calls out Grant when he slips back into a joking mode about sex. He will speak up about what's bothering him without the overriding fear that he will lose the relationship. He no longer pesters Grant to keep talking about their disagreements for hours. He can let things go for a while and get back to them the next day if it still feels like an issue. He's doing more things on his own now, too, without feeling the anxiety he used to feel when Grant was busy with his own friends and hobbies.

Grant:

Grant believes that sex should be easy, and if you need to talk about it, something must be wrong. He comes into their relationship with a certain amount of confidence, and it shakes him to find out Tom has things he likes that are different than what Grant has been doing in his previous relationships. He struggles with anxiety and resistance during the exercise because it is uncomfortable for him being the Giver without that sense of confidence he was used to.

Once he shifts his perspective, Grant comes to love hearing from Tom about what he wants. All the pressure is off him to know what to do or to be an expert. His self-consciousness disappears because he knows Tom must be getting what he wants if that's what he is asking for. Giving becomes easy and joyful for him because all he has to do is follow directions. He loves seeing Tom happy. That is so different than the fear he used to see in Tom's eyes at the mention of sex. Their sex life has been so strained for so long, and Grant has never seen Tom abandon himself and just really be happy. He quickly feels hopeful and positive about their sex life because he can shift to thinking about himself and his own pleasure.

Grant mostly stops joking about sex, although he slips occasionally. He's able to be direct about what he wants. Now that

Tom is enjoying sex and doesn't seem afraid, Grant is having an easier time initiating again.

Grant has also gotten much better about handling his anger and reacting with moderation. He's broken his family's pattern of inflicting big emotions on the people you love. He's also staying involved in their discussions and disagreements. He'll take a time out when he needs one, but he will circle back and make sure they finish their conversation.

Grant and Tom have much more open communication about sex at this point. They have both developed the ability to know what they want and put it into words. They handle conflict better, with a balance between sticking it out until things are resolved but also taking breaks or setting the disagreement aside when their talks aren't productive. They are both feeling less shame about sex and about their sexual orientation. They are also having penetrative sex at this point. They did research about it, talked about it a lot, and gradually experimented with how it would work best for them. It's a regular part of their sexual repertoire, although they still find a lot of pleasure in other forms of sexual interaction. They recently got engaged.

CHAPTER 12

What's Next?

Congratulations! Sex without stress doesn't mean there isn't still a lot to tolerate, but you are now more able to tolerate what is there. You can take the pressure off your sex life and make it fun. Where sex was hard, you can now make it easier, if not downright simple.

You have covered a lot of ground in the course of this book. Whether you've taken the time to work through the various steps as you read about them or whether you've read the book to understand what to do when you're ready, you now see how there can be a progression from avoidance and pressure to lightness and fun.

The ideas and process that I outline in the book are the same ideas I cover with clients who attend my private practice. I walk you through the same concepts and exercises that have helped hundreds of couples improve their sex lives.

The first stage of the process is to gain understanding, about both the problematic cycle that has you trapped as well as how sex and relationships can work better with a new mindset. You come to see how your unrealistic expectations set you up for feelings of failure, how those feelings result in avoidance of sex, and how that avoidance increases the pressure you feel. I encourage you to embrace a concept of sex that emphasizes connection and pleasure. I want you to expand your sense of what sex is and what success looks like. By addressing your expectations and then laying out some new rules of the court for you and your partner to play by, you are set up to approach sex in a way that you cannot fail.

The next stage of the process is about working with your partner to gain insight into your issues and where they come from. You learn how to talk to your partner about your joint struggles with sex. You explore your family dynamics, your sexual history, and your past relationships to recognize what comprises your baggage and where you got it. You look at the various factors that make your sex life even more complicated. You deconstruct the dance you and your partner perform around having (and not having) sex. You wrap this part of the process up by figuring out what your individual role is in perpetuating the problems. You understand what you need to think and do differently to make improvements in your relationship.

The last stage of the process is action. You develop and practice the ability to behave differently with your partner. You use the Giver/Receiver Exercise, the hands-on tool that allows you to practice all these new behaviors and strategies. You learn about how the exercise works and how to use the information you get from doing it for continuing progress. You see that the process of having physical experiences while you focus on your own improvement gives you a chance to practice and grow. The exercise is a laboratory where you can gradually test and recalibrate your thinking and your actions about sex. You work through nine different phases to attain a stress-free sex life, focusing on one at a time, until you are able to master all nine phases and apply them simultaneously.

To help you apply the concepts, I describe the progress of four different couples as they navigate this process. You meet them when they are completely stuck in the Avoidance Cycle, each for their own reasons. You see their process of discovery as they figure out why they are stuck and what each person is contributing to the problematic dynamics. You hear about their experiences with the Giver/Receiver Exercise—both the challenges and the successes. Each couple is much happier and more relaxed in their sex life now that they've done this work.

I have written the book to get this information and strategy into the hands of the people who need it, not just the people who can enter therapy. This is a do-it-yourself book. That creates two challenges. You have to do it. By yourself. If you could work through this process with a therapist, you would have a professional to provide guidance, support, structure, and accountability. Doing this on your own will require commitment, determination, and stamina. I realize it's a tall order to work through all this material and all the iterations of the exercise that it will take to change your sex life, especially if you encounter difficulties or questions. I've done what I can in the book to help you see that the struggles are common and normal. I have worked to instill hope in order to encourage you. I have devised a process that you can follow to make change, setting it up so that you can take small steps and feel progress along the way. But you may not have someone to help you navigate the resistance that comes with the territory of improving yourself and your sexual relationship. You may not have an easy way to find motivation if you struggle (although I have listed a couple of my favorite books in the resources section at the end). You may not have someone to consult about the questions you have. I am developing several other offerings and programs specifically to try to help you through the process. If you want more support in your journey, I hope you will access these resources, listed below, as they become available.

Thank you for spending this time with me. I hope you enjoyed the book, but even more, I hope the ideas and exercises have been helpful in improving your sex life. I would like nothing more than to help people intimately connect with their partner. It is my sincere wish that you have discovered pleasure and connection with your partner. I want the days of disappointment, avoidance, and pressure to be a thing of the past, and sex to feel easy and joyful. I trust that you can see the light at the end of the tunnel if you haven't started yet or are still in the midst of this process. A happy, fulfilling sex life and relationship is possible if you and your partner want it, work on it, and maintain it.

MORE SUPPORT IS ON THE WAY.

This book is just the first step in providing resources to people looking to improve their sex lives. To support you on this journey, I am developing several tools and programs that complement the book. If you'd like to keep up to date with what is being released, I invite you to visit my website, *www.jessazimmerman.com*, and join my mailing list. That way, you'll be alerted as these new offerings are released. The site is also where you'll find links to these resources.

Here's a look at some of what's coming:

An online course

An online course based on the ideas in this book is currently under development. If you're a person who does better with interaction and guidance to keep you motivated to make progress, an online course will be perfect for you. Or if you're someone who learns through auditory and visual means, rather than through books, this may be of interest. The course will use videos, lessons, and worksheets to help you move through the process with your partner, giving you a structure to the process.

Workshops and retreats

Live workshops and multi-day retreats are being developed. They will help couples move through this process in an intense and focused way. Retreats will be designed to move through the material covered in the book, with time to have the conversations and experience the exercises. Held in beautiful settings that encourage relaxation and focus, the retreats also give you a chance to ask questions and get guidance as you work through the process.

A free Facebook group

I host a free online group through Facebook called Sex, Intimacy & Relationships. There, I share articles and items of interest, I facilitate conversation, I answer questions, and I broadcast live with ideas and information that could help your sex life. My goal is to create community among people who are committed to creating their best possible intimate relationship.

A card "game"

I will be developing a set of cards to use as a tool to expand your intimate life. The set will be appropriate and useful for all kinds of couples, regardless of gender, sexual orientation, physical ability, and anatomy. It's meant to be an open-ended and customizable system for increasing touch and eroticism. It allows the users to delve into what's pleasing and erotic to them instead of following prompts generated by someone else. It will be a great tool for learning to access desire and explore eroticism.

An online erotic quiz

Look for an online quiz geared toward discovering your own eroticism and how it overlaps with a partner. It will provide insight into your sexuality as well as ideas about how to share your interests with a partner.

A private membership group

I will be launching a private membership group. At a low monthly cost, this membership will be a way to get the support and guidance you may need to follow through with the process, as well as a way to be able to interact with me. It will include a private, members-only webpage with exclusive content, regular live coaching and Q&A sessions, community and conversation with others working on their sex lives by way of a private Facebook group, and first access and discounts to other programs.

RESOURCES

Sex, Orgasm, and Masturbation

Anderson, D. (2008). *Sex Tips for Straight Women from a Gay Man*. New York: HarperCollins.

Castleman, M. (2004). *Great Sex: A Man's Guide to the Secret Principles of Total-body Sex*. Harlan, IA: Rodale.

Dodson, B. (1996). *Sex for One: The Joy of Selfloving*. New York, NY: Three Rivers Press.

Erickson-Schroth, L. (Ed.). (2014). *Trans Bodies, Trans Selves: A Resource for the Transgender Community*. New York, NY: Oxford University Press.

Foley, S, Kope, S. & Sugrue, D. 2nd edition. (2012). *Sex Matters for Women: A Complete Guide to Taking Care of Your Sexual Self*. NY: Guilford Press.

Heiman, J. & LoPiccolo, J. (1987). *Becoming Orgasmic: A Sexual and Personal Growth Program for Women* (Revised expanded ed.). New York, NY: Fireside.

Joannides, P. (1997, 2007). *Guide to Getting It On* (9th ed.). Oregon, USA: Goofy Foot Press.

Kerner, I. (2004). *She Comes First: The Thinking Man's Guide to Pleasuring a Woman*. New York, NY: HarperCollins.

Ladas, AK, & Whipple, B. (2005). *The G Spot: And Other Discoveries about Human Sexuality*. New York, NY: Dell Pub. Co.

Leight, K. A. (2013). *Sex Happens: The Gay Man's Guide to Creative Intimacy*. Minneapolis, MN: Langdon Street Press.

Mintz, L. (2017). *Becoming Cliterate: Why Orgasm Equality Matters-and How to Get it*. New York, NY: HarperCollins.

Morin, J & Moris, J. (2010). *Anal Pleasure and Health: A Guide for Men, Women, and Couples*. U.S.A.: Down There Press.

Nelson, T. (2008). *Getting the Sex You Want: Shed Your Inhibitions and Reach New Heights of Passion Together*. Beverly, MA: Quiver.

Newman, F. (2004). *The Whole Lesbian Sex Book: A Passionate Guide for All of Us* (2nd ed.). San Francisco, CA: Cleis Press.

Resnick, S. (1997). *The Pleasure Zone: Why We Resist Good Feelings and How to Let Go and Be Happy.* Berkeley, CA: Canari Press.

Siverstein, C., Picano, F. (2003). *The Joy of Gay Sex* (3rd ed.). New York, NY: HarperCollins.

Vernacchio, A. (2014). *For Goodness Sex: Changing the Way We Talk to Teens about Sexuality, Values, and Health.* New York, NY: Harper Wave.

Weiner, L. & Avery-Clark, C. (2017). *Sensate Focus in Sex Therapy: The Illustrated Manual.* New York, NY: Routledge.

Zilbergeld, B. (1999). *The New Male Sexuality: The Truth about Men, Sex, and Pleasure* (revised ed.). New York, NY: Bantam.

Relationships

Chapman, G. (2015). *The 5 Love Languages: The Secret to Love that Lasts.* Chicago, IL: Northfield.

Diamond, D., Blatt, S., & Lichtenberg, J. (2007). *Attachment and Sexuality.* New York, NY: The Analytic Press.

Easton, D., & Hardy, J. (2009). *The Ethical Slut: A Practical Guide to Polyamory, Open Relationships, and Other Adventures.* San Francisco: Greenery Press.

Fisher, Helen. (2004). *Why We Love: The Nature and Chemistry of Romantic Love.* NY: Henry Holt.

Gottman, J. (1999). *The Seven Principles for Making Marriage Work: A Practical Guide from the Country's Foremost Relationship Expert.* New York, NY: Random House.

Hendrix, H. (2007). *Getting the Love You Want: A Guide for Couples* (20th Anniversary ed.). New York, NY: Henry Holt & Company.

Johnson, Sue. (2008). *Hold Me Tight: Seven Conversations for a Lifetime of Love.* New York, NY: Little, Brown & Company.

Karen, Robert. (1998). *Becoming Attached: First Relationships and How They Shape our Capacity to Love.* NY: Oxford University Press.

Lawrence, E., Rothman, A.D., Cobb, R.J., Rothman, M.T., and Bradbury, T.N. (2008). "Marital Satisfaction Across the Transition to Parenthood." *Journal of Family Psychology, 22,* 41-50.

Taormino, T. (2008). *Opening Up: A Guide to Creating and Sustaining Open Relationships.* San Francisco, CA: Cleis Press, Inc.

Veaux, F., Rickert, E. (2014). *More Than Two: A Practical Guide to Ethical Polyamory.* Portland, OR: Thorntree Press.

Werrbach, M. (2014). "Predicting Divorce: The Four Horsemen of the Apocalypse." *Psych Central.* Retrieved on November 24, 2017, from https://psychcentral.com/blog/archives/2014/07/06/predicting-divorce-the-four-horsemen-of-the-apocalpyse/

Communication

Christensen, A. & Jacobson, N. (2002). *Reconcilable Differences.* New York: Guilford Press.

Stone, D., Patton, B., & Heen, S. (2000). *Difficult Conversations; How to Discuss What Matters Most.* New York, NY: Penguin Books.

North Seattle Community College. *The Interpersonal Gap.* Retrieved on January 27, 2018, from http://faculty.northseattle.edu/wholt/bus236/lessons/s02files/ip_gap_2.pdf.

Mind Mapping

Schnarch, D. (2018). *Brain Talk: How Mind Mapping Science Can Change Your Life & Everyone in It.* New York, NY: Sterling Publishers.

Religious Upbringing

Sellers, T. S. (2017). *Sex, God, and the Conservative Church: Erasing Shame from Sexual Intimacy.* New York, NY: Routledge.

Infidelity

Glass, S. (2004). *Not "Just Friends": Rebuilding Trust and Recovering Your Sanity after Infidelity.* New York, NY: Free Press.

Nelson, T. (2012). *The New Monogamy: Redefining your Relationship after Infidelity.* Oakland, CA: Hew Harbiner.

Perel, E. (2017). *The State of Affairs: Rethinking Infidelity.* New York, NY: HarperCollins.

Spring, J. A. (2012). *After the Affair: Healing the Pain and Rebuilding Trust When a Partner Has Been Unfaithful* (2nd ed.). New York, NY: HarperCollins.

Snyder, Douglas K., Baucom, D.H., & Gordon, K.C. (2007). *Getting Past the Affair: A Program to Help You Cope, Heal, and Move On—Together or Apart.* NY: Guilford Press.

Sexual Desire

Diamond, Lisa. (2008). *Sexual Fluidity: Understanding Women's Love and Desire*. MA: Harvard Univ. Press.

Foley, Sallie. (2005). *Love and Sex for Grown-ups: A No-Nonsense Guide to a Life of Passion*. NY: Sterling Press.

Kaufman, S. B. (2017, July 19). "The Science of Passionate Sex: How to Have Hot Sex, According to Science." [Blog post] Retrieved from https://blogs.scientificamerican.com/beautiful-minds/the-science-of-passionate-sex/

Kort, J. & Morgan, A. (2014). *Is My Husband Gay, Straight, or Bi?: A Guide for Women Concerned about Their Men*. Lanham, MD: Rowman & Littlefield.

Love, P. & Robinson, J. (1995). *Hot Monogamy: Essential Steps to More Passionate Intimate Lovemaking*. New York, NY: Plume.

Nagoski, E. (2015). *Come as You Are: The Surprising New Science that Will Transform Your Sex Life*. New York, NY: Simon & Schuster.

McCarthy, B & McCarthy, E. (2009). *Discovering Your Couple Sexual Style: Sharing Desire, Pleasure, and Satisfaction*. New York, NY: Routledge.

Metz, M. E., & McCarthy, B. W. (2011). *Enduring Desire: Your Guide to Lifelong Intimacy*. New York, NY: Routledge.

Mitchell, S. A. (2002). *Can Love Last?: The Fate of Romance Over Time*. New York, NY: Norton.

Resnick, S. (2012). *The Heart of Desire: Keys to the Pleasures of Love*. NJ: Wiley & Sons.

Schnarch, D. (2011). *Intimacy and Desire: Awaken the Passion in Your Relationship*. New York, NY: Beaufort Books.

Schnarch, D. (2009). *Passionate Marriage: Keeping Love and Intimacy Alive in Committed Relationships*. New York, NY: W.W. Norton & Company.

Tripp, C.A. (1987). *The Homosexual Matrix* (2nd ed.). New York, NY: McGraw-Hill.

Sexual Dysfunction

Birch, RW. (1997). *Male Sexual Endurance: A Man's Book about Ejaculatory Control*. Pec Pub.

Goldstein, A, Pukall, C & Goldstein, I. (2011). *When Sex Hurts: A Woman's Guide to Banishing Sexual Pain*. MA: Da Capo Press.

Levine, Laurence. (2008). *Understanding Peyronie's Disease: A Treatment Guide for Curvature of the Penis*. Omaha, NE: Addicus books.

McCarthy, B., & Metz, E. (2004). *Coping with Erectile Dysfunction: How to Regain Confidence and Enjoy Great Sex*. Oakland, CA: New Harbinger.

McCarthy, B., & Metz, E. (2004). *Coping with Premature Ejaculation: How to Overcome PE, Please Your Partner and Have Great Sex*. Oakland, CA: New Harbinger.

Schnarch, David. (2002). *Resurrecting Sex: Resolving Sexual Problems in Your Relationship*. New York, NY: HarperCollins.

Aging

Barbach, L. (2000). *The Pause: Positive Approaches to Menopause*. New York: Plume/Penguin.

Block, JD & Bakos, SC. (1999). *Sex Over 50*. Upper Saddle River, NJ: Prentice Hall.

Price, Joan. (2011). *Naked at Our Age: Talking Out Loud about Senior Sex*. USA: Seal Press.

Ward, R., Rivers, I., & Sutherland, M. (Eds.). (2012). *Lesbian, Gay, Bisexual and Transgender Aging*. Philadelphia, PA: Jessica Kingsley Publishers.

Trauma

Davis, L. (1991). *Allies in Healing: When the Person You Love Was Sexually Abused as a Child*. New York, NY: HarperCollins.

Lew, Mike. (1988). *Victims No Longer: Men Recovering from Incest and Other Sexual Child Abuse*. New York, NY: Nevraumount.

Haines, S. (2007). *Healing Sex: A Mind-Body Approach to Healing Sexual Trauma*. San Francisco, CA: Cleis Press.

Haines, Staci. (1999). *The Survivor's Guide to Sex: How to Have an Empowered Sex Life after Child Sexual Abuse*. San Francisco, CA: Cleis Press.

Levine, Peter. (1997). *Waking the Tiger: Healing Trauma*. Berkeley, CA: North Atlantic Books.

Maltz, Wendy & Holman, Beverly. (1987). *Incest and Sexuality: A Guide to Understanding and Healing*. Lexington, MA: Lexington Books.

Maltz, W. (2012). *The Sexual Healing Journey: A Guide for Survivors of Sexual Abuse* (3rd ed.). New York, NY: HarperCollins.

NiCarthy, Ginny. (1997). *Getting Free: You Can End Abuse and Take Back Your Life*. Seattle, WA: Seal Press.

Van der Kolk, B. (2015). *The Body Keeps the Score: Brain, Mind, and Body in the Healing of Trauma*. New York, NY: Penguin Books.

Zolbrod, Aline. (1998). *Sex Smart: How Your Childhood Shaped Your Sexual Life and What to Do about It.* Oakland, CA: New Harbinger Pubs.

Illness and Disability

Albaugh, Jeffrey. (2012). *Reclaiming Sex and Intimacy after Prostate Cancer: A Guide for Men and Their Partners.* NJ: Jannetti Publications Inc.

Alterowitz, R. (2004). *Intimacy with Impotence: The Couple's Guide to Better Sex after Prostate Disease.* Boston, MA: DeCapo Press.

Katz, A. (2009). *Sex When You're Sick: Reclaiming Sexual Health after Illness or Injury.* West Port, CT: Praeger.

Kaufman, Miriam, Silverberg, Cory, & Odette, Fran. (2003). *The Ultimate Guide to Sex and Disability: For All of Us Who Live with Disabilities, Chronic Pain and Illness.* San Francisco: Cleis Press.

Laken, Virginia & Laken, Keith. (2002). *Making Love Again: Hope for Couples Facing Loss of Sexual Intimacy.* Sandwich, MA.: Ant Hill Press.

Grief and Loss

Nathan, Edy. (expected 2018). *It's Grief; the Dance of Self-Discovery Through Trauma and Loss.* NY: As I Am Press.

Body Image

Alvear, M. (2013). *Not Tonight, Dear, I Feel Fat: How to Stop Worrying about Your Body and Have Great Sex: The Sex Advice Book for Women with Body Image Issues.* Naperville, IL: Sourcebooks.

Cash, Thomas. (1997). *The Body Image Workbook: An 8-Step Program for Learning to Like Your Looks.* CA: New Harbinger.

Pornography

Maltz, W., & Maltz, L. (2009). *The Porn Trap: The Essential Guide to Overcoming Problems Caused By Pornography.* New York, NY: Harper.

Eroticism

Bader, Michael. (2003). *Arousal: The Secret Logic of Sexual Fantasies.* New York, NY: St. Martin's Press.

Barbach, L. (Ed). (1995). *Erotic Interludes: Tales Told by Women.* New York: Plume/Penguin.

Barbach, L. (Ed). (1988). *Pleasures: Women Write Erotica.* New York: HarperCollins.

Bering, J. (2013). *Perv: The Sexual Deviant in All of Us.* New York, NY: Scientific American / Farrar, Straus and Giroux.

Friday, N. (1998). *My Secret Garden: Women's Sexual Fantasies.* New York: Pocket Books.

Kahr, B. (2008). *Who's Been Sleeping in Your Head: The Secret World of Sexual Fantasies.* New York, NY: Basic Books.

Morin, J. (1995). *The Erotic Mind: Unlocking the Inner Sources of Sexual Passion and Fulfillment.* New York, NY: HarperCollins.

Perel, E. (2007). *Mating in Captivity: Unlocking Erotic Intelligence.* New York, NY: HarperCollins.

Wiseman, J. (1998). *SM 101: A Realistic Introduction.* San Francisco: Greenery Press.

Mindset and Motivation

Hendricks, G. (2010). *The Big Leap: Conquer Your Hidden Fear and Take Life to the Next Level.* New York, NY: HarperCollins.

Olson, J. (2013). *The Slight Edge: Turning Simple Disciplines into Massive Success and Happiness.* Austin, TX: Greenleaf Book Press Group.

ABOUT THE AUTHOR

Jessa Zimmerman is a licensed couples' counselor and nationally certified sex therapist. She works in private practice in Seattle, WA. Over the course of her therapy career, she has focused almost exclusively on helping couples with their emotional and sexual intimacy.

In her years of clinical experience, Zimmerman has treated hundreds of couples who have struggled to feel sexual desire and fulfillment. Her clients describe having a good relationship in other ways, but their sex life has become difficult to the point that they start to avoid sex. These are people who love each other but are struggling to have a sex life they both enjoy.

She specializes in helping these couples who find that sex has become stressful, negative, disappointing, or pressured. She educates, coaches, and supports people as they go through her 9-phase experiential process that allows them real world practice in changing their relationship and their sex life.

Zimmerman received her Master's in Psychology from LIOS college of Saybrook University and Sex Therapist certification from the American Association of Sexuality Educators, Counselors, and Therapists (AASECT). She has done extensive training in couples' therapy, with a focus on Crucible® Therapy with Dr. David Schnarch.

She is the host of the Better Sex Podcast and has appeared on numerous other podcasts as an expert guest. She hosts the Sex, Intimacy & Relationships group on Facebook and broadcasts live on a regular basis.

She lives in Seattle with her partner and youngest child of three.

Made in the USA
Monee, IL
01 August 2023

40305295R00111